BOOMERS!
(A Survival Guide for the Future)

By

Dr. Evan Keliher

Pedagogue Press P.O. Box 28808 San Diego, CA 92198

Copyright 2007 Evan Keliher

Cover Design by Steve Lopez, Hemet CA

All rights reserved, no part of this book may be reproduced or transmitted in any form or by any means, electronic or mechanical, including photocopying, recording, or by any information storage and retrieval system without written permission from the author, except for the inclusion of brief quotations in a review.

ISBN: 978-0-9648859-7-4
SAN: 298-8054

Library of Congress Catalog
Card Number: 2007929050

Printed in the United States of America

Other works by Evan Keliher

Books

Grandpa's Marijuana Handbook
Guerrilla Warfare for Teachers
The De-Balling of America
Grandpa Ganja's High School Survival Guide

Videos/Films

Rebel High (feature film)
Montreal, Canada
My Lovely Bank (sitcom pilot)
Montreal, Canada
Grandpa's Marijuana Handbook (the movie)
San Diego, CA

Stage Plays

Sandwiched Light
Witte's End

See additional plays/screenplays/sitcoms
www.grandpaspotbook.com

Table of Contents

	Intorduction	7
1.	Who Are We?	10
2.	How to Get to Be Old	15
3.	Exercise	21
4.	Diet	28
5.	Freedom	33
6.	Seniors and Sex	38
7.	Should You Marry Again?	51
8.	Voting	59
9.	Old-timers and Crime	61
10.	Children/Grandchildren	71
11.	Second Careers	77
12.	Money/Investments	85
13.	Dressing Right	92
14.	Plastic Surgery	99
15.	Travel	104
16.	Condos/Clubs	110
17.	Driving (Cheating)	118
18.	Sleeping	124
19.	Divorce	131
20.	Religion	137
21.	Canes, Walkers, Etc.	144
22.	Shoplifting Seniors	150
23.	Anti-Aging Tactics	157
24.	Drugs/Booze and Sobriety	163

25.	Wills	171
26.	Old Folks' Homes	176
27.	The Problem of Dead Friends	183
28.	Suicide	189
29.	Last Words	202
30.	Funerals, Etc.	208
31.	The Summing Up	217

INTRODUCTION

At seventy-six, I've been a senior citizen for fourteen years. It's official. When I turned sixty-two the government certified me as a bona-fide senior citizen entitled to all the rights and privileges appertaining thereto. I collect Social Security, my health insurer is some outfit called Medicare, and I get senior citizen discounts at the movies. If there are any other official perks, I don't know what they are.

What's that? You say you were born between '46 and '64? So that makes you a Boomer, doesn't it? It also means you're getting older. Everybody who doesn't die is getting older with every breath he draws. In fact, instead of complaining about it you should rejoice since the only alternative to aging is dying and none of us is in any hurry to do that, is he?

Remember, only the lucky ones get old. Check the obituaries and note the fate of those who've found a way to beat old age. You'll see a lot of people in their forties and fifties who keeled over on golf courses or drove their cars into trees or succumbed to some exotic disease rather than face the perils of age. These people will never have to deal with the problems of growing old, but at what a price?

Consider yourself lucky. It's an honor to be old, a privilege not given to all. Be glad about it. Stand up tall—or as tall as you can, anyway—and look the young whippersnappers in the eye and tell them you're glad to be ninety years old and to get the hell out of the way before you run them over with your walker, by God!

Old age is a highly desirable state and it always has been. People in all societies have always revered old age and longed to hang onto life at any and all costs because life offers so many more options than death does.

Think about it. Living people can take walks and watch TV and smoke cigars and eat, drink, and be more or less merry while dead ones are pretty much limited to lying about and waiting for vague Second Comings that may or may not come to pass. On the whole, it appears that being alive is preferable to being dead and most of us seem to know this fact instinctively judging by the tenacity with which we cling to life.

It's not enough just to live, though; it matters how you live. The secret is to make it to a hundred or so and have some fun in the process, to do it with style and grace and as much class as you can muster. It's important that the years count, or what's the point of it all?

I wrote this excellent book as a kind of how-to manual to provide a little much needed guidance for the fifty- or sixty-million people in this country who are either already old-timers or well on their way to such a state. These can be the best years of your life if you only know how to make the most of them, and this book will help you do exactly that.

So we'll analyze this aging business from stem to stern, as they say, and see if we can divine a course of action that'll help us get through the experience. We'll examine its various aspects in no particular order and report our findings as we uncover them. Above all, we'll strive for candor and truth and call them as we see them. After all, it's the least we can do.

Remember, age is good, the older the better. Fight the Grim Reaper to the very end; refuse to give up. Trick him if you can, bob and weave, offer a moving target. The object of the game is to stay alive as long as possible by any means fair or foul; the game's over when you show up on Grim's computer printouts at last and he comes round to collect your defunct carcass.

CHAPTER ONE

Who Are We?

There was a time when people only lived to be twenty or so. Lions ate them or the crops failed and they starved to death or the neighbor in the next cave came over and bashed their brains out or whatever, but something got them before long and they only managed to average a twenty-year life span. Everyone wanted to live a long time, of course, but not many were able to pull it off.

This was still true in ancient Greece and Rome where the average life expectancy was thirty or thereabouts. While it's true that fewer people were being eaten, starved or bashed by this time, they still died off from ruptured appendixes, various infections, and the odd plague. They knew almost no science back then and relied entirely on such notoriously ineffective cures as magic potions and the intercession of priests praying to non-existent gods.

It was tough on people then. Consider the following scenario. A guy goes to his doctor with a pain in his side. The doctor is cutting a farmer's hair but he stops long enough to give the guy the once over.

"I've got bad news, Bob," the doctor says. "It's your appendix. I'd say she's ruptured on you."

"Ruptured? Is that bad?"

"Yep. Looks like you're a goner, Bob."

"Well, can't you do anything?" Bob says.

Doc shrugs. "What can I do? Nobody's invented surgery yet. We don't even know about anesthesia or the circulation of the blood or the details of the germ theory. I'd tell you to go home and take two aspirins but..."

And there you have it. Bob goes home and dies from an ailment that any registered pharmacist could cure in a trice today. That's what comes of being born anytime prior to the arrival of the 20th century and the advent of modern science. How can anyone expect to live a long and fruitful life sans x-rays and penicillin and vitamins and an understanding of the dangers of cholesterol in high-fat diets?

Modern science has done a spectacular job in coming up with newfangled devices and schemes to keep us living longer and better lives. They've got steel ball-bearing knee joints, transplanted livers and hearts and kidneys, open-heart surgery, laser treatments, drugs for impotent guys, glass eyes and plastic limbs and wonder drugs and on and on in a veritable cornucopia of modern medical miracles.

Such knowledge lets us enjoy much longer life spans than ever before in our history. The Japanese average eighty years, the Germans are close behind, and almost everybody else is in that same neighborhood. Some South American Indians live to be a hundred or more and can run up and down mountains like so many goats well into their second century. And some Russians in the Caucasus Mountains are robust and vigorous at equally lofty ages.

Of course, these people manage to stay alive so

long only because they live in unheated mountain cabins and walk miles to town every day and live on yogurt and turnips and earn their living as peasant farmers and lumberjacks but, what the hell, you can't have everything. After all, would you rather be dead?

One question that often comes up is what is old age, anyway? How do you know when you've reached it? Is it when you qualify for senior citizen discounts? Is it a certain arbitrary age like sixty or eighty? Is it a condition like the inability to get it up? Or is it merely a state of mind, something indefinable and capricious and personal?

The truth is it's all of the above. The first time the ticket girl at your local movie theatre cheerily suggests the senior citizen's discount you'll feel ancient even if you're only forty-five. In fact, you'll feel even worse to know you look sixty when you're still in your forties.

When you qualify for Social Security you'll be reminded officially by the government that you're now classified as an old-timer and entitled to public assistance whether you need it or not. You may go around telling everyone you feel forty or so and regularly play tournament tennis and have a keen interest in the opposite sex, but you'll still be an old person in the eyes of the government.

If there is an arbitrary age when you may be said to be old, that age is sixty-two. After all, who can argue with the government? If Congress says you're old, well, then, it must be so. With the average American living to be about seventy-five, you'll only be a dozen years from that ultimate rendezvous with Charon and his infamous boat. While sixty-two may not be really old in many cases it's close enough to serve as a guideline for our purposes here.

Of course, age is relative in many ways. We all know people who seem old at forty and others who defy age at eighty. It's at least partly a mind-set, a mental attitude, one we can control to a very large degree if we're determined enough. You can just refuse to grow old, refuse to be a party to any of it and insist you're still young and fit in spite of all evidence to the contrary.

I myself am an example of this defiance. A year after I'd retired from teaching school in Detroit I went to the annual luncheon of the Retired Teachers Society and was appalled at what I saw assembled there. The place abounded in derelicts. The youngest appeared to be about eighty-six or so and none of them was able to get up or sit down without help. I took one look at this bunch and resolved I'd never have anything to do with such people again. And I never have, either.

Other examples of this are to be seen everywhere. The octogenarian who climbs Mt. Everest on his eightieth birthday; the centenarian who remembers voting for Teddy Roosevelt and is launching her campaign for Congress; an old colonel who starts a chicken empire with his first Social Security check; all are people who refused to accept the label of old and continued to go right on living with vim and vigor when they could not reasonably be expected to do so.

The point is age really is relative. It's only a

number, a general indicator; a kind of numerical road sign alerting us that we're at a given point on our collective ways to dusty death. Taken by itself it means nothing; it has exactly as much meaning as we choose to give it.

What all this means is that life ends when we die and not a minute sooner. Intelligent people know this and insist on living life to the fullest no matter what their age.

I suggest you do the same.

Survival Rules
1. For a long life move to the Caucasus Mountains.
2. Confine your diet to hearty peasant food.
3. Old age officially begins at sixty-two. Rejoice that you're around to have it happen to you.
4. Avoid really old people lest you be mistaken for one of them.
5. Old age is ultimately nothing more than a number; have the courage to sneer at it.

CHAPTER TWO

How to Get to Be Old

As we've already seen, it's not all that easy to get old in the first place. Maybe nobody wants to die en route to old age but a lot of them do, anyway. While it's true that living to be eighty or ninety has much to do with luck, still there are certain strategies that have worked for millions of others and can work for you, too.

Take the luck part first. What's your DNA look like? Do you come from a long line of octogenarians or did all your ancestors drop dead in their early forties? We're talking pure luck here; nobody controls his own DNA. If your luck is bad you're just out of luck, I guess.

Were you born in a slum or teething on the fabled silver spoon? If you were unlucky enough to draw the slum, you've had fewer of life's luxuries such as sound medical care and a decent diet and your overall health may have suffered as a result.

On the other hand, if your folks were rich you've had all these things and your health should be in somewhat better shape generally. Fewer rich kids end up with TB or dietary deficiencies and consequently more of them reach maturity in fairly good health. In other words, it's always better to be rich than poor because the rich people not only have more money but they also enjoy better health and out-live the rest of us.

I'm not sure, but somehow that doesn't seem quite democratic, does it?

Then there's the element of luck in avoiding fatal accidents along the way. You can be the healthiest person in three counties and get run over by a bus at thirty. What good is health to a dead guy? We're talking luck again. Some people are just plain luckier than others, that's all. One guy pilots jetliners all over creation for thirty years and never gets a scratch and the next guy takes his very first plane ride at forty and the thing slams into a mountain.

People would say the crashee had bad luck—and he surely did.

Any fool can see, then, that luck plays a key role in determining who gets to eighty and who doesn't. For some of us it just isn't in the cards no matter what we do on our end. All the dieting and exercising and vitamins and physical exams and medicine in the world aren't worth a damn if we're not a bit lucky, too.

What about the strategies? What can we do to stave off the Grim Reaper as long as possible and make it into our dotage along with the rest of the winners?

For one thing, choose a safe and sane career. Don't choose life as an infantryman in a Marine rifle platoon. Avoid stuntman work. Stay away from such jobs as deep-sea diver, sponge fisherman, and abalone farmer. In fact, stay out of the oceans altogether, as there are all sorts of things in them that will eat you at the very first opportunity.

Don't be an undercover narcotics cop or a steeplejack or an inner-city public schoolteacher or a firefighter or an intravenous drug user or anything else that has a known high mortality rate. It's tough enough living to be eighty without handicapping yourself with some death-defying career.

The jobs you do want would include accountant, retail sales, government bureaucrat, hairdresser, librarian, fashion model, symphony conductor, research scientist, housewife, and similar jobs renowned for their low health risks. Symphony conductors all live to be ninety or so and most librarians routinely live to be a hundred or more. (This can be verified by examining the lives of people like Arturo Toscanini and dropping by the nearest library and noting the old ladies one sees there.)

As for particular strategies, you can learn tried and true survival methods by talking to old-timers who've managed to stay alive for eight or nine decades and know a trick or two about how it's done. For example, I ventured out to the Sunny Dale Old Folks' Home and did some research among the inhabitants there to get some insight into the problem.

One old codger glared at me with his one good eye while its glass mate gazed vacantly at the ceiling and said, "Secrets? You bet I got some secrets. It's hard work, that's what it is. A man should put in at least twelve hours a day six or seven days a week and never take a vacation. Makes a guy too tired to think about death, he won't have any time for it. If people don't work hard, they die off early. Keepin' busy, that's what it takes."

Of course, this guy's testimony was not all that reliable since the old fool's mind was half gone and he had no idea what he was talking about. I later learned he was a retired preacher and had only worked on Sundays for the last fifty years. Still, there are those who claim hard work is good for you and will prolong your life.

On the other hand, I interviewed an old lady who was nearing a hundred and she took the opposite tack.

"Constructive leisure, young man, that's the secret," she said. "Don't do any work at all if you can help it. Marry a rich man like I did. Surround yourself with laborsaving devices and do a lot of shopping. Shopping is especially good as it gives a person something to live for. And take separate vacations. You won't get any rest if you take your old fool of a husband along with you."

With that she cackled loudly and zipped off in her electric wheelchair without a backward glance.

Others there recounted similar stories and they were as diverse as these. Where one old geezer claimed careful diet attributed to his longevity another swore he lived entirely on nicotine, caffeine, and fat grams. Some pleaded for exercise and others claimed they never broke a sweat in ninety years. One visited her doctor regularly and underwent more surgeries than a lab rat while her equally old roommate avoided doctors and medicines and depended on natural herbs and tonics made from dandelions and berries.

They tell us there are some things we can do to prolong our lives such as eating less red meat, avoiding excessive drinking, not smoking, and getting enough exercise. All these are well-known factors in assorted afflictions from heart attacks to cancer and fatal falls.

And then along comes some joker like Winston Churchill, a renowned trencherman who routinely ate red meat, drank copiously, smoked a dozen or more cigars every day, never exercised a single day in his life, and lived into his nineties. What kind of message does that send to the rest of us?

In fact, the more I probed this aspect of longevity the more I learned that there doesn't seem to be any one method for arriving at an advanced old age. People seem to get there by a variety of routes. One that would prolong your life might kill me outright while my preferences would deliver you to an early grave.

Again, the key components to attaining a long life seem to have more to do with the aforementioned DNA and old-fashioned luck than anything else. If you can avoid those encounters with careering Mack trucks and have inherited the right genes, you can reasonably expect to live well into your eighties or nineties and spend your declining years attending the funerals of your less fortunate friends.

I guess the best course of action for most of us is to do pretty much what we want to do without being foolish about things. Eat what you want, drink or smoke as you like. Run, jog, or take long naps as suits your particular disposition and generally forget about it. We all die of something sooner or later and excessive worrying about it is likely to make it sooner rather than later.

Survival Rules
    1. To live a long life, be lucky and have good genes.
    2. Be born rich in an industrialized nation with a good health care system.
    3. Avoid fatal accidents.
    4. Choose a safe career: accountant, librarian, or a symphony conductor.
    5. Live abstemiously.
    6. Or do exactly what you like and rely on your karma and the gods.

CHAPTER THREE

Exercise

Everybody's always telling us we ought to exercise more on the grounds that it's good for us and will prolong our lives indefinitely. Even as a teenager I doubted that there was much to this theory and I studiously avoided exercise at every opportunity, but I really knew they were full of crap when Jim Fixx died while jogging.

Here was this man who wrote books on the lifesaving benefits of arduous exercise and practiced what he preached by running a dozen miles or more every day. He was lithe and lean, the consummate runner, a model of the well-exercised form—and he dropped dead of a heart attack at fifty-two.

Is there a message here or what?

I read of a study done at Michigan State University once that found college varsity athletes lived not a minute longer than the average Joe based on actuarial charts. And the average life expectancy for pro football players is fifty-three. What? The jocks don't outlive the rest of us? Their highly developed cardiovascular systems and well-muscled bodies break down right on schedule with those of the nerds and pencil necks?

Incredible.

The plain truth of the matter is there's no real benefit in being hot and tired and out of breath for any reason. Once you're out of your teens, you should confine your activities to those that don't call for any unusual exertion. If you run around out in the hot sun chasing after assorted balls and whatnot, you can expect to dislodge an aneurysm or pop an aorta and it'll serve you right, too.

Listen, this exercise craze is not only a lot of hokum but there really is a good chance it could also be fatal. Fixx isn't the only guy that's heart burst on him due to excessive strain brought on by violent exercise. Read the papers. People are dropping all over the place. Paramedics make regular runs to so-called health studios and haul away heart patients and stroke victims who collapsed while on the rowing machine or suffered a seizure while bench pressing several hundred pounds of iron.

See for yourself. Go to any health club and hang around the place for an afternoon and you're bound to see at least one old codger fall down and turn blue from overexertion. It's so common a sight that most regular customers go right on with their workouts and take no notice of the drama unfolding before them.

"Hey, Cartwright's down again!" the assistant manager sings out. "Better call 911—and order us a pizza while you're at it."

They administer mouth-to-mouth resuscitation and pound on the guy's heart and he's whisked away by the paramedics and never seen on the premises again. The papers will run a two-paragraph story next to the underwear ads on the local news page and that's all anybody ever hears of it.

Don't you become a player in a similar scenario.

Avoid exercise. Refuse to join the local joggers' association. Resign from the tennis and swim club forthwith. Sell your bowling ball and dump those golf clubs. Eliminate all forms of strenuous exercise from your daily routine and you'll be better off for it.

Now this isn't to say that all exercise is bad for you. On the contrary, certain sensible types of exercise come highly recommended, especially for old-timers like you and me.

Take sex—and you should, as often as you can get it. You profit from this activity in at least two ways. First, there are actual aerobic benefits to be gained. If you take it seriously and really put your whole heart and soul—and other appropriate parts—into the act, you'll gain enormous benefits in terms of your overall health.

More importantly, an active sex life promotes health in more subtle ways, but we'll examine these in a later chapter.

It's okay to walk. Sauntering is even better. Resting and sleeping are even better yet. Lolling about is also good. Watching TV with your feet propped up on an ottoman, a cold beer in one hand and a hand-rolled cigar in the other is a universally recognized form of exercise that's rigorous and demanding enough to meet all your needs. Why do more when you can get by nicely on so much less?

If you have friends who are into such foolishness as jogging or playing tennis and you want to go along to be sociable, that's okay as long as you don't actually join in and run the risk of incurring the aforementioned aneurysm or popped aorta. The secret is to play the role without straining yourself.

Suppose you fall in with a bunch of joggers and they beg you to join them in their madness. Okay, you feign enthusiasm. Tell them you've always admired long-distance runners and have long wished you could become one yourself. Carry a picture of Jim Fixx in your wallet. Make vague references to anabolic steroids and hint that you're familiar with their use.

Go out and buy jogging clothes. Get some skin tight, polyethylene pants with racing stripes and wear a headband. Buy some fancy sneakers, the kind that enable you to jump higher and farther than Michael Jordan. Watch track and field events on TV and refer to them in your conversations with fellow joggers.

In short, play the part to the hilt. They'll welcome you with open arms and you'll have a whole array of new friends and a greatly enhanced social life in no time at all.

Just don't do any jogging.

How do you get out of it? Easy. When the gang is getting together to jog up the face of Mt. St. Helens or whatever, you show up in all your jogging regalia—and using a cane. This scene will unfold.

"Hey, Mabel, what happened? What's with the cane?"

"I'm afraid I've pulled a ligament," you say, giving your calf a stout whack with the cane out of pure frustration at such wretched luck.

"Oh, no!" someone will say.

"How terrible!" another will declaim.

"Yep, she's torn, all right," you reply. "I decided to take a warm-up run yesterday and I was half way up Heartbreak Hill when the damn thing snapped on me." Snap your fingers. "She went just like that. I gave her a shot of steroids and soaked her all night but it's no use. I guess I'll have to sit this one out."

"Oh, what a shame," they'll exclaim.

"Hey, why don't you ride with Shirley and help with the picnic lunch?" someone will say, and a chorus of sympathetic friends will join in and urge you to come along as a non-participant and you're home free.

And there you have it. You're functioning in a jogger's club and gaining all the social benefits therein without actually jogging as much as a single yard. Of course, you can easily come up with similar dodges when your torn ligament "heals" and sustain the fraud endlessly.

Claim you've broken your Achilles' tendon. Hint that you're a candidate for open-heart surgery and reinforce the deception by popping what you claim are nitroglycerine tablets but are really M&Ms. Say you're suffering from painful shin splints or your arthritis has kicked in again or all that shrapnel in your back from World War II is acting up.

In other words, be creative. You should be able to hang out with joggers indefinitely and never work up a sweat. You can harangue your friends with endless tales of jogging stories and hint that you're considering running in a marathon soon and gain the admiration and respect of people everywhere and all the time you couldn't run to the corner and back without the aid of a portable oxygen tank and a trained physical therapist.

You can do the same with all other kinds of exercise, too. Lots of people belong to tennis clubs and never swing a racquet. Skiers often buy elaborate outfits and expensive, custom-made skis and never leave the sanctity of the ski lodge with its roaring fireplace and hot toddies. Swimmers get great tans and never enter the water.

But surely you get the idea by now. Exercise is not beneficial for the average old-timer. On the contrary, it's contra-indicated for most of us once we've grown to adulthood and should be indulged in only under extreme circumstances.

Of course, it's all right to run madly about if you're trapped on the twenty-fifth floor of a major hotel fire or to swim two miles through a raging surf if your boat has capsized on you and the alternative is a watery grave, but otherwise avoid exercise if at all possible. Avoid placing undue stress on a heart already weakened by age, cholesterol, and years of riotous living.

So take the easy way out. Even if you don't actually live as long as the exercise freaks, you'll have a helluva lot more fun in the time that is allotted you.

Survival Rules
   1. Remember Jim Fixx.
   2. Stop exercising when you leave your teens.
   3. Avoid health clubs as undesirable types hang out in them.
   4. Get lots of sex for the aerobic benefits.

5. Enjoy pseudo-exercise by watching the pros on TV while smoking a cigar and drinking a beer.
6. Wear neat sports outfits and $100 Nikes but evade actual exercise by faking injuries.
7. Remember, there's no advantage in being tired and sweaty.

CHAPTER FOUR

Diet

What about eating? Are there special Boomer diets that will help you get old and stay that way for two or three decades? Is it true you can eat your way to an early grave as the health nuts claim?

Yes and no. Lots of evidence today shows that diet plays a major role in the kinds of diseases we develop over the years. This is especially obvious when we compare other countries with our own. The Japanese eat less red meat than we do and it's been shown they suffer less from cholesterol and heart trouble as a result. The aforementioned Caucasus Russians subsist on nuts, goat cheese and fruit and they almost never die.

The average American's diet is probably not the best one for achieving advanced old age. We're heavy on fat grams and don't eat enough vegetables. A lot of us drink milk in spite of numerous studies indicating it wreaks havoc on adults and should be avoided altogether by everyone over twelve or so. Pork is loaded with fat that converts directly to artery-blocking sludge within fifteen minutes of consuming it and we eat about fifty million pigs each and every year as a nation.

You should also avoid exotic fare such as banana and peanut butter sandwiches, as the chemical reactions of certain combinations are unpredictable and may produce unexpected results. Remember Elvis?

Cheese is another fat-laden comestible and yet we eat the stuff by the ton on our pizzas and cheeseburgers. Mexican food is loaded with fat of all kinds and we scarf it down with reckless abandon. Ice cream and chocolate cake and candy and apple pie and other rich desserts round out the average American's diet and contribute to early death and/or life-threatening obesity for millions of us.

Still, you've been luckier than the others. You've managed to grow old in spite of such diets and now you're an old-timer well into your fifties, sixties, seventies and the question now is, what's diet got to do with you at this stage in life?

Answer: Nothing. Who cares now? You're old and way up on Grim's printouts and subject to call at almost any moment and you're worried about what you eat?

The point is nobody lives forever. I don't care if you live entirely on grains and fruits and life-giving mineral water, you're still on your way out and there's not a damn thing you can do about it. And if that's true, there's only one sensible course open to you.

Forget it. Eat whatever you like. Get fat. Cut loose and live a little before it's too late. You're going to come a cropper in any case so you may as well go for it and let the devil take the hindmost.

This diet business is all well and good when you're young since good eating habits will help you get old, but there comes a point where diminishing returns become a factor. What have you got to gain by continuing to eat health-giving foods when you're eighty-years old, for God's sake? Is there any sense in that? You'll gain little and lose much by denying yourself whatever you want in the way of comestibles.

To see what old-timers actually did about this, I interviewed randomly selected people on city streets and asked them if they'd made a practice of watching what they ate earlier in life and whether they continued with such practices now that they were old.

I approached an old lady who was pushing one of those walkers down the sidewalk at a snail's pace and put the question to her.

"Oh, dear me," she said, "yes, I certainly do watch what I eat. I eat only fruit and whole grains, no meat at all. And lots of prunes, too. And fibre."

"But don't you find such a regimen a little boring?" I asked. "Don't you ever long for a hamburger or sundae or a slab of ribs?"

"Young man, you don't get to be ninety-two by eating ribs and ice cream," she snapped. "So what if your food tastes like cardboard? Staying alive is what counts and don't you forget it!"

She glowered at me and took off up the street in pursuit of several snails that'd just raced by her and a minute later she tried a daring move on the snails and keeled over dead right in front of a Burger King.

Talk about irony.

A fat old guy stopped to gawk at the fallen dieter and I put the same question to him.

"What?" he said. "Diet? Does it look like I'm on a diet? I'm eighty-eight years old and you want me to watch my weight? What the hell for? Do I look like I'm headin' for a swingin' singles bar? You think I'm on my way to a health club? Diet? Are you crazy? I'm headin' for a fat 'burger, that's where I'm goin'."

And with that he scooted around the fallen woman and ducked into the restaurant to stock up on fat grams and caffeine.

Now this gentleman takes a more sensible approach to eating. He's already an old-timer and on the verge of imminent death with little to lose. He took care of himself all those years and lived on a lot of bland stuff and walked around hungry half the time in order to live a long life. Okay, so he succeeded. He's eighty-eight and still upright. So what's he saving himself for?

He knows Grim's just around the corner and heading his way at this very minute. The jig is almost up. He's denied himself and lived an ascetic life and now he should cut loose and make up for lost time. Order a second fat 'burger, replenish the fries, make it a large coffee, real coffee with extra caffeine and double sugar. Always have dessert. Pack it in. As I said, what are you saving it for?

What does it matter if your corpse looks like Henry the VIII? So what if people make snide remarks at the viewing?

"My, but he put on a lot of weight, didn't he?"
"He got fatter'n a pig is what he did."
"Yeah, he looks like Henry the VIII."
"They're gonna need extra pallbearers to get his fat ass outta here!"

Who gives a damn? Believe me, you won't.

The point is, there's a time for caution and a time for wild abandon and the wise person knows the difference. The old lady could have been scarfing 'burgers and chocolate shakes for the last several years and not been any the worse off for it in the end.

So the secret is to watch what you eat when you're younger and chow down when you get old and are running out of time.

Survival Rules
1. For the first sixty years eat less not more. Avoid red meat, milk, and rich desserts.
2. After sixty eat whatever you damn well please. Savor caffeine. Load up on refined sugar. Choose foods by fat gram—the more the better. Enjoy what's left, for God's sake!

CHAPTER FIVE

Freedom

One real advantage of being a very old person is that it gives you the freedom to be anything or do anything you like without worrying much about the consequences. After all, if you're seventy- or eighty-years old what more can anybody do to you? What the hell, the Grim Reaper is probably checking his computer printouts and making inquiries about you already and you can't be in more serious trouble than that, can you?

I knew one old guy who always wanted to learn to fly a plane but he was afraid to do it because the damn things are always falling out of the sky and crash landing on freeways and into the sides of buildings. At thirty or even fifty, he just wasn't ready to take the risk of being killed prematurely.

Then he turned seventy and he hurried right down to the local airport and signed up for flying lessons. When I asked him what finally gave him the nerve to go ahead with it he said, "Because I'm seventy-years old, that's what. What can happen to a guy my age? I'll be a goner anyway in four or five years so I may as well go out in a blaze of glory."

Now, that's a laudable attitude and I told him so. Unfortunately, the wings fell off the plane the first time he went up and the poor sap was killed but the moral of the story is still valid. There's much less to lose when you're old and that justifies the taking of greater risks than you might take at twenty. So live it up. If you don't like something, speak up about it. Let people know you don't give a damn. All your life you've had to think of the consequences when you were tempted to voice your true opinions about something and now you no longer have to do that.

Suppose you're standing in line somewhere and some clown cuts in front of you. Do you suffer in silence? Do you mutter under your breath and glare meaningfully at the back of his head? Like hell you do.

"Hey!" you shout. "I'm talkin' to you, stupid! Yeah, you! Get in back of the line! Who the hell do you think you are, anyway?" And so on.

The sap will crawl to the back of the line like a whipped puppy, as you continue to harangue him for the amusement of the crowd. What else is he going to do? You're ninety-years old and look it. Is he going to attack you? An enraged crowd would fall on him and beat the crap out of him if he assaulted such an old lady. Or even an old man. What bully would fight a ninety-year-old, even if the old guy was a real pain in the ass and deserved a sound thrashing?

Your advanced age protects you. Nobody wants to be seen abusing our most senior citizens; it's bad for one's image. And this doesn't apply just to bullies since anyone abusing the elderly automatically looks like—and is—a major jackass. This even extends to officials of various kinds who share these views.

Judges are inclined to go easy on old-timers hailed before their courts because of the image thing.

Remember Abbie Hoffman? He told you to steal his book. I go him one better and tell you to steal food if you're hungry. If you shoplift a ham, say, or run amuck in the produce department of the local supermarket, the judge is reluctant to give you hard time because he dreads the story in the papers the next day showing him sentencing a feeble old geezer to jail.

In fact, you can get away with just about anything if you're old enough. Shove a box of fine stogies in your shopping bag and make a run for it. If they catch you pretend to have a heart seizure and surreptitiously drop a handful of your lawyer's business cards around the place. Insist you've been set up, that a masked man ordered you to steal the stogies or he'd harm your children (who are all into their sixties now but that's beside the point). Raise a lot of fuss. Insist that the names of all bystanders be taken as potential witnesses in the upcoming trial when you sue the storeowners and their heirs and assigns in perpetuity.

Play your cards right and the manager will let you keep the stogies if you'll just promise to shut the hell up and get out of his store.

You can talk to yourself on the street and people will only smile knowingly. After all, you're old and therefore a bit balmy so such behavior is all right, even expected. You can drive twenty miles-an-hour on busy freeways, take all day to park, lose your car in the parking lot and demand the store send a stock boy out to find it for you and it's all okay because you're a harmlessly befuddled senior citizen.

If you're lucky enough to be a hundred or so you

can do anything short of actual murder with impunity. Break out of the old folks' home and terrorize neighborhood pool halls and the legal system will smile benignly. Run up behind pretty girls in the park and pinch their derrieres and people will applaud your spirit, as lascivious conduct in centenarians is regarded as cute. Smoke cigars in the lobby of La Valencia hotel in La Jolla and defy anyone to stop you, by God!

See how it works? The older you get the more real freedom you have. There are almost no limits for very old people. The idea is to know this and take advantage of it.

Lots of people, maybe most of them, become more conservative as they get older. They switch from the Democratic Party to the Republican, from frolicking to frowning, from men-about-town to couch potatoes. They slow down on sex and invest in blue chip stocks and buy four-door sedans. Worst of all, their minds atrophy on them, the synapses snap like so many brittle rubber bands and the whole brain shorts out and they're unable to deal with anything that happened after 1960.

You have to resist this. Remember, time's running out, the end draws near and you hear the faint rustle of printouts in the background. It's time to live as you've never lived before. Do outrageous things. Take wild chances. Hang out down at the docks late at night. Try to find a waterfront saloon where Bogart, Sidney Greenstreet, and Peter Lorre provide local color. Make a study of massage parlors and report your findings to your fellow octogenarians.

All this is possible because you're so old it doesn't matter anymore what you do or how you behave. People will make allowances for you. For the first time in your long life you're actually free. You can do anything—and you should.

While it's true there aren't a whole lot of pluses to advanced age, still there are some and it behooves you to take advantage of them where and when you can. Don't limit yourself to senior citizen discounts at the movie houses when you can be yourself at last and never be held to account for it. Spread those wings, realize long-lost dreams, put a little fun in your life and hang the consequences. You're invulnerable at last.

It's odd somehow that we should only get true freedom as we stand at death's door, but that's how it happens. So, what the hell, be free at last.

It is your last chance, you know.

Survival Rules
1. Old age brings the ultimate freedom. Enjoy!
2. Fear nothing or no one.
3. Nobody wants to abuse senior citizens as it makes them look bad. Take advantage of this.
4. Flaunt the law and defy them to do anything about it.
5. Take chances—Grim is gaining on you.

CHAPTER SIX

Seniors and Sex

What?! A chapter on old people and sex? Aren't the two incompatible? Is sex and the aged even a subject to be discussed by respectable people? Isn't it all just a bit embarrassing, a bit, well, unseemly?

A lot of people think so, but none of them is an old-timer. People in their thirties and forties think sex is inappropriate for elderly folks, but the old-timers have a different slant on things. It's always easy enough to tell other people how to conduct their sex lives—or even if they should have sex lives—but it's quite another thing when they're being encouraged to adopt celibacy.

Who started this idea, anyway? Why does everyone think sex is something to be reserved just for those under sixty? Does the first Social Security check mean you're finished, that you'll never get it up again? Does it mean you can no longer entertain a prurient thought? Does your libido wither and die as you open the envelope and shake out that check?

The answer is hell, no!

Sex is a lifetime proposition and it should last as long as you do. You can rightfully think sexual thoughts, and even act on them, until Grim catches up to you on that fateful day. Sex is too good to confine to the young; besides, young people never truly appreciate it the way oldsters do because the young regard it as a routine affair with unlimited charges still left in the works while old-timers know it's a limited commodity and every time out may well be their last.

So don't let them stifle your normal, healthy interest in good old-fashioned sex. Of course, there are certain things which will tend to lower your sex drive as you get much older, things like the inability to get it up for you guys out there. This can be a very traumatic experience for the average guy.

When you're used to summoning the Little General on command, or even having him show some initiative and appear on a whim of his own, and then you find it increasingly difficult to get him to stand at attention at all it can be a hard thing. (Actually, this isn't the best choice of words since it's lacking a hard thing that causes all the trouble, but you know what I mean.)

The first thing you want to do when you notice a flagging interest on the General's part is to make sure nobody's putting saltpeter in your food. You remember that stuff from your army days; it's a chemical that prevents erections. A daily dose of saltpeter in your pancakes and you couldn't get the damn thing up with a block and tackle, for God's sake. Some guys went through whole wars without getting laid even once because their systems were chock full of saltpeter.

How would you encounter this noxious stuff now that you're no longer under your government's direct control? Easy. Are you married? If so, keep an eye on your wife. Wives have been known to feed their horny husbands saltpeter by the peck to keep them from wanting more sex than they want to give them.

In fact, some experts estimate that at least half of all cases of impotence are caused by wives using saltpeter as a condiment unbeknownst to their husbands who naturally tend to attribute their loss of libido to age.

Anyway, it's worth checking out so send a sample of the mashed potatoes or pea soup to a reliable chemist and have it analyzed. If you do find saltpeter the only solution is to dump your wife. Any woman so depraved as to poison her husband in this way is beyond redemption and should be sent packing at once.

Of course, the advent of Viagra has altered the rules some. If a man can still get it up his sex life will continue apace—or should. The only problem for most guys is finding a willing partner who can keep up since wives are infamous for refusing to hold up their end of things. Some obvious solutions to the problem offer themselves but I won't go into them here since my wife is liable to read this stuff.

Both sexes need to be careful that the negative attitudes of others don't creep into their own thinking re sex and cause them to give it up on the grounds that it's immoral or improper for them because they're old. If you show any interest in sex as an old-timer your kids may profess to being embarrassed and suggest you "act your age." Get rid of these kids.

This is especially true if you're single. Your kids will discourage you from dating and roll their eyes heavenward at any suggestion of carnal thoughts on your part.

"Mother, you can't be serious!" daughter will

say when you announce your plans for a weekend trip with the old codger in the next condo. "What will people say? How can you even think of such a thing when poor old dad's only been gone for eighteen years?"

Et cetera.

Tell them to get lost, by God. What business is it of theirs if you get a little from time to time? Are they really worried about what people will say? Or are they more concerned that you may do something stupid like marrying the old codger and thereby louse up their rightful inheritance?

Go on that weekend!

Women should spiff up their wardrobes and dress with an eye to recapturing some of that old sex appeal they once had in abundance. Wear low-cut blouses and see if you can still stand in high heels. Show some cleavage and flash a little thigh. Talk sexy. Tell risqué jokes and load up on double-entendres. Mystify them. Lay in a supply of artificial pheromones to replace the real ones you've lost and trail a cloud of the stuff everywhere you go.

If there are any men left alive where you live, single one out and go after him with all your feminine wiles. Show up on his doorstep holding a freshly baked apple pie with an erotic scene carved in the crust to get the guy's attention. Tell him hula dancing is your hobby and offer to show him a few moves. You don't actually have to know how to dance the hula, of course; once you get him alone and put a few moves on him he won't give a rap about dancing.

But what to do if there aren't any living men within reach? Suppose the only guys you ever see are in their nineties and not of much use in the man department. What then? You'll have to get yourself one of those self-help manuals and look after your own affairs.

Trot on down to your neighborhood adult bookstore and ask to see their selection of dildos. (Don't pick up any of the guys you find hanging around those places, though, as they tend to be an odd lot and will disappoint you.) Spend a little more and get an electric one, the kind that runs on batteries so you can take it with you in the car or to the theatre.

Get assorted sizes and pretend you're the star attraction at a stag party. Don't be afraid to fantasize bizarre things, places, people. Be Cleopatra or a porn star or a black-gartered hooker or the neighborhood hussy working her way through a house party somewhere in Middle America.

Stock up on exotic underwear; get some with lace and uplift bras. Buy skirts with slits in them. Long slits. Wear nylons with garter belts. In other words, if it's true that you are what you pretend to be then pretend to be somebody who's still interested in sex. What the hell, it's all in your mind anyway, isn't it?

Plastic surgery? Should old-timers have it done in their seventies and eighties? Why not? Look what surgeons did for Cher and Robert Redford. Modern science can do the same for you and you should take advantage of it or else what's it for?

Besides, if you have some deficiency like

overwrought thighs or sagging buttocks, how would you hope to correct them? Join a health club and work it off? Don't be ridiculous. Remember the chapter on Exercise?

No, the only sane answer is the surgeon's knife. What? You say there's some risk in surgery? So? You're an octogenarian, who cares? Sign up for liposuction. Let them hook up that fat sucker and start work on those buttocks—and don't stop there. Tighten up that tummy and draw up that neck and raise that face to Old Glory. Cap your teeth if you have any of the originals left.

If your boobs have fallen too far to be lifted by anything short of a large forklift, consider plastic surgery for a new set of knockers. A set of big, bold knockers would look silly on an old lady? Who says so? You'll hear no complaints from the guys on this score, believe me. All guys admire and respect nice boobs and some of it's bound to rub off on the proud owner of same.

So shore up your drooping cheeks and sandpaper your forehead and have them retrofit everything else while you're at it. Make a whole new you, don't stop until you can pass for fifty again and then get out there and hunt those widowers down as you did in days of yore when the saps were young and so were you.

As for you saps, you can also benefit from the miracles of modern medicine. Lots of men have plastic surgery done these days, everything the women do and more. There's one particular bit of surgery that every guy should consider when the time comes, and that's one of these penile implants they've got now.

You know how they work. You find out one day that your donniker's suffered some sort of mechanical failure and the Little General refuses to stand at attention anymore. What's worse, the little slacker won't even come to parade rest. Needless to say, the word will soon spread and you'll be a laughingstock of all the widows in the neighborhood and an object of derision and scorn—and rightly so. What sexually active woman wants an old geezer around if he can't get it up?

Well, your troubles are over. Just hie yourself down to the local urologist and tell him you want a new donniker. Some of the newer models even let you specify size within limits and this will be an added inducement for those of you who've gone through life with a pitiful six- or seven-incher.

There are two basic models, one that's more or less permanently at attention and another that you work with a pump and inflate like a tire at your own convenience. Most guys opt for the pump because they naturally choose the jumbo size replacement model. If they get the permanent one it encourages endless Mae West jokes about the gun in their pocket.

For those averse to surgery we now have wonder drugs like Viagra that will get the General's attention with a single pill and keep it long enough to get the job done and done right. The stuff is safe overall but there are a few caveats. For one thing you could get something called priapism, an erection that won't go away when you no longer require its services. Although this may seem like a good thing at first glance, it's not. Keep the erection too long and it may explode from pent up energy and injure passersby.

One way to restore normalcy is to have sex continuously for the next four hours but this will only work if you have enough willing partners to help out. Even with available partners your wife will flatly refuse to let you have sex with six or seven beautiful girls; she'd rather see the damn thing explode. That means you'll have to hurry on down to the emergency room to deflate it.

Anyway, just think how your life would change if you were walking around armed with a Little General that would stand at attention on command and stay that way until you let the air out of him. Talk about popularity! Why, every widow, grass and otherwise, would be after you with all her available charms. You'd have enough pies to open a bakery. You could go from condo to condo and leave a raft of satisfied women in your wake. You'd be written up in the condo newsletter, asked to speak at women's luncheons, besieged by love-stricken women from sixty- to ninety-years old and generally spend your declining years in Aphrodite's arms where all men have always longed to be.

Even more, you'd be regarded as a philanthropist of sorts, a man who unselfishly sacrificed himself to add pleasure to the drab lives of others. What could be more commendable? More praiseworthy? More honorable? Or more fun?

Again, the secret is to stay active sexually. Most

people fall into indifference because they get bored with conventional sex and they're too worried about what the ubiquitous busybodies will think if they do anything irregular. And it's even worse for the senior citizens since people have so stereotyped them as sexless creatures that they're half ashamed whenever a stray erotic thought shows up.

That's wrong. Sex is normal and natural throughout life and no one needs to apologize for his sex life as long as it involves consenting adults. And that means old people can have it with all the vigor and enthusiasm of teenagers.

But back to that healthy interest. Keep active. If you're bored after fifty-odd years of the missionary position, dump those missionaries and look through the Kama Sutra for some fresh ideas. Introduce your partner(s) to the wonders of the Sumatra Head Stand or the Burmese Joint Coupling Maneuver and gain a whole new outlook on sex as it can be sans inhibitions.

Announce your interests in things sexual by subscribing to Playgirl or Penthouse and leaving copies lying around for guests to see. Keep a shelf of X-rated DVDs in full view. A whip tossed casually over a chair, a pair of spiked high heels idling in a corner, a Little Bo Peep costume atop a pile of clothes awaiting cleaning, all will broadcast your interest in carnal matters and encourage others who share those interests to say so.

You might see something like the following. The handsome old duffer across the way enters your condo to bring you the latest newsletter and he spots your whip.

"Oh, say, that's a mighty nice whip you've got there," he says.

"Oh, that old thing!" you say. "I've had it for years. They last forever, you know. Why, I've beaten men from coast to coast with that whip and it's as good as new."

"From coast to coast, eh?" he says, a gleam in his eye that wasn't there a moment ago. Then he espies the X-rated DVDs and he moves toward them with mouth agape. "X-rated stuff, eh? Boy, you've got some classics here. Sally and the Seminary Students, The Car Hops Hop Alpha Sigma, Coeds Invade the Locker Room..."

"Hey, I not only collect them, I've even starred in a few," you say, reaching for one of the tapes. "Now this one right here, I did this last year. It's called Bar Girls in San Diego. It's got a lot of sailors in it. Want to see it?"

Of course he does. You shove it into the DVD player, slip on those spiked high heels, do a Zorro number with the whip, and you've got yourself an afternoon frolic just like that. Neat, eh?

Another good idea is to join a group with whom you have a common interest. One such group could be the local chapter of Peeping Toms of America, Inc., a non-profit outfit of guys who meet for nightly forays into the neighborhood to window peep together. All you need are some first-class binoculars, the kind you can see in the dark with, if possible, and some dark clothing so the peepees won't spot you on the roof or wherever.

These guys will be guys just like you, guys drawn together by an interest in voyeurism and looking at naked women. You'll likely find a judge or two, several scoutmasters, a teacher, a Rotarian, at least one preacher and several members of his flock, and assorted others from similar backgrounds. They'll know all the really hot spots where the action is and they'll be glad to show them to you.

You'll need a certain amount of dexterity, too, and fairly decent night vision since Peeping Toms spend a lot of their time scampering around high-rise buildings at midnight in order to gain the best vantage points. They shimmy up and down fire escapes like so many mountain goats and think nothing of hanging by their heels from overhangs eight- or ten-stories above terra firma in their quest for unwitting ecdysiasts.

Or you could sign up with a nearby chapter of foot fetishists and go with them to shoe conventions. You'll find the very same sort of people into foot fetishism as you'll find in window peeping. Sure, it's true a lot of them are podiatrists or shoe salesmen or stocking manufacturers, but there are lots of dentists and cops and accountants, too.

Foot fetishists are very social people and they often get together in private parties where they regale each other with sexually stimulating stories having to do with footwear. They bring their collections and have contests with prizes for best heel in a pump or slinkiest sling back. At the close of each party they break out the champagne and a solemn toast is drunk from a wide assortment of ladies' shoes.

Or you can affiliate yourself with a neighborhood flashers' group and pop in and out of bushes with your pals and wave your donniker at passing ladies. It's an inexpensive hobby, too, as your only outlay is the cost of a long coat. It's also convenient as you can do it anytime day or night with very little effort on your part. There are no dangerous fire escapes to climb, no shoes to buy, and little chance of getting caught.

Still, some of you guys might want to think this one through before you run down and join up. Remember, the point here is to menace women with your donniker and a lot of you wouldn't be considered a menace by anything female. How would it look if you showed up at a meeting and begged admission and they asked you to undergo initiation? You don a coat, step forward, and shake your donniker in a menacing manner—and the room erupts in laughter!

See what I mean? Make sure you have menace potential before you aspire to the flashers.

But you get the idea. Do whatever is necessary but keep up your normal, healthy interest in sex as long as you can. It's not only all right to do so, it's crucial that you do. And turn a deaf ear to anybody who even suggests you're too old for sex.

Such a thing isn't even possible.

Survival Rules
1. Remember, you're never too old for sex!
2. If you guys can't get it up, check for saltpeter in your food.
3. Get a penile implant and become the toast of

your condo.
4. Ladies should invest in a supply of artificial pheromones to replace those lost.
5. Memorize the Kama Sutra.
6. Stress variety. Stock up on whips, Bo Peep costumes, and whipped cream.
7. Get active in social groups like the window peepers, fetishists, and flashers.
8. Stock up on Viagra.
9. Remember, you're never too old for sex!

CHAPTER SEVEN

Should You Marry Again?

Okay, so you're in your seventies or eighties and you're single. There's no shame in that, especially in these times, since just about everybody seems to be living alone now. The divorce rate is so high it's a wonder anybody's still married by the time they get old, and damn few of them are to their first mates.

People do get divorced and many of them more than once. Serial monogamy has replaced the former kind throughout Christendom; in fact, it's likely monogamy as we knew it will never more be seen in these parts. It's an anachronism in the 21st century, a quaint idea whose time has come and gone only to be replaced by...what? God knows.

Okay, so your most recent mate has passed on, gone to his reward, kicked the bucket, bought the farm, crossed over, or, in a word, died. Or you've endured your most recent divorce, trial separation, desertion, and now find yourself alone. It's lonely out there when you're alone, so lonely your mind plays tricks on you and tries to lead you to commit rash acts in an effort to set things right. Things like getting married again, for example.

Don't you do it, by God!

Consider. You're on your own and you're dating somebody. This other party (male or female, fill in the blanks) wants to get married and you're tempted. However, Alzheimer's hasn't gotten you yet so you can still think and you go home and get a pad and pencil and do just that. And what do you discover?

First, you realize there are significant economic factors to consider. Do you commingle property? How do you know the scoundrel/bitch isn't a crook that goes around the country marrying half-wits like you and making off with all their money? It happens all the time and not always to other people.

What about your heirs? Are you going to marry this person and die two months later and have him/her scoop up your entire estate as your beneficiary and leave your own family high and dry? Do you think there aren't people out there hoping for that exact scenario as they waltz you down the aisle?

What's worse, some of them are even willing to play an active role in your departure. Hardly a day goes by that you don't read where some vicious old bat has been marrying and murdering husbands for their insurance money and burying their carcasses in her back yard. In either case, the situation cries out for caution. Think about it.

But even assuming your intended isn't a serial killer or an adventurer after your money that still doesn't mean marriage is the thing for your average octogenarian. Consider further.

You know how they say people get set in their ways, as they get older? Since almost nobody's older than you, it follows that your ways are firmly set in cement and absolutely immovable. You know it's true, don't you? And yet you'd marry another old codger like yourself whose ways are as immovable as your own?

So the guy smokes cigars and you hate cigars. He isn't about to quit so that means you have to live in a house that stinks like the backroom at an old-time political convention? You think you can handle that?

Or she's a talker, one of the non-stop kind that rambles endlessly about nothing at all and hypnotizes herself with the sound of her own voice. Marriage? You can't be serious.

Or he never wants to leave the house and you love to go out. Or she hates the outdoors and you love camping and fishing. He drinks and you're a teetotaler. She's a culture hound and you're a sports nut. He's an early riser and you like to sleep in. She gave up on sex years ago and you never get enough.

See? Look at all the adjustments you have to make just to have somebody around. Is it worth it? Almost never.

This person is going to be a pain in the neck and a major nuisance in a dozen different ways if you marry him/her. Your life will never be your own. It'll mean constantly humoring the old fool, putting up with eccentricities that would unhinge Mother Teresa. Is this something you want to do at eighty?

And what about the kids? Remember the threatened inheritance? The kids on both sides will be pissed with both of you because they fear for "their" money. And they fear with good reason, I might add. We've all heard of countless cases where the old man fell under the spell of some gold-digging witch who attached herself to Dad like a lamprey eel to a trout and sucked the old guy drier than one of Keating's savings and loan shops.

Naturally, the kids are going to bitch and they should. Some hussy sweeps in and confounds some old geezer who hasn't had a clear thought in years before she arrives on the scene and she gets him to sign everything over to her the day before he croaks. Does anyone, other than the hussy, that is, think this is right? Of course not.

So, if you marry again you're going to get lots of flack from both sides and that's going to be another sore spot to add to all the others. As you already know, it's hard enough to make any marriage work under the best conditions, so starting out with all these minuses will make success almost impossible.

This brings us to the best reason of all for not marrying anybody when you're old. I'm talking about playing nurse for years on end when this old duffer suffers a major stroke or heart attack or outbreak of Alzheimer's and ends up a permanent patient with you in charge of his care.

Think about it. When you date people in their seventies and eighties you're dealing with folks at the end of the trail, folks who are subject to major breakdowns just by virtue of the fact that they're old. It's one thing if you've been married for years and your spouse requires extensive care, but it's something else again when you find you've taken on that responsibility for someone you hardly know.

Another thing involves economics again. You could become legally responsible for this guy's care and end up spending everything you have to keep him ensconced in the Sunny Dale Old Folks' Home for fifteen or twenty years while he waits for the Grim Reaper to show up and there goes the aforementioned inheritance you were saving for your own kids.

So don't do it.

Okay, does this mean you can't form permanent relationships with others? Not at all, you can eat your cake and have it, too. It just means you must be circumspect in what you do.

Why not just live in sin? You're a Boomer, aren't you? This is the 21st century. Cohabit. Shack up. Take in a roommate. Split expenses but each of you keep your own stuff in your own name. In fact, get a prenuptial agreement that spells out your intentions so there won't be any bizarre claims later when one or the other dies or otherwise moves on. In other words, thanks to Lee Marvin, you can forget all about this palimony crap.

Will your kids be pissed because you're living in sin? If they are just offer to marry and watch them back off in a hurry. They'd much sooner have you sin your aged heart out and have to spend eons in purgatory than see their inheritance eaten up by the people at Sunny Dale or sucked up by the hussy.

What about the rest of society? Will people blacklist you socially if you shack up? Are you kidding? If anything it will add an aura of glamour and provide panache hitherto unknown to you. You'll be perceived as a free thinker, chic, a swinger.

"Oh, did you hear about Elga? They say she's got

a new boyfriend. Moved in last week."

"Elga? She's shacking up? Why, who'd have thought it? I never figured her for such a swinger. Let's call her up and invite her to our bridge club for lunch."

"Good idea. She can fill us in on all the juicy details."

The point is we're operating under new rules now. Nobody gives a damn for all that crap about getting married and having the proper licenses and permits and approval of a lot of goofballs at City Hall who are all engaged in exotic sexual aberrations of their own, anyway. People make their own rules today; it's even cool to do so.

Better yet, don't even cohabit. It's a lot less complicated if you each keep your own place and just sleep over when the mood strikes. You can keep toothbrushes and bathrobes in each place and that makes it easier when one of you has that stroke. No need to call a moving van and stand around awkwardly while your furniture is trundled away as your erstwhile paramour watches with tear-filled eyes from his sick bed. You just grab your toothbrush and robe and duck out the back door when he isn't looking and that's that.

That's cruel, you say? We lack compassion? We're heartless? Nonsense. We're just being realistic. Nobody should have a lifelong claim on you just because you spent a few months together in an informal relationship short of marriage. There wasn't any of that in sickness and in health malarkey this time around; you made no promises and neither did he. You agreed to stick together through thick and thin and when it gets too thick you thin out. What's wrong with that?

Of course, guys are lucky since our society is so structured that it's quite acceptable for very old men to marry quite young, even nubile, women (girls) and then the risk of having to nurse someone is greatly reduced. Most nubile young women are not susceptible to strokes and other debilitating afflictions and you could easily enjoy six or seven years of marital bliss before that stroke fells you and she has to take care of you.

Unfortunately, our society won't really allow older women to marry much younger guys and work the same scam. Not only that but most guys tend automatically to look for women much younger than themselves and I don't blame them. Given the choice between marrying Grandma Moses and a starlet most guys will invariably choose the starlet. Is this fair? Certainly not, but so what? That's how it is.

So there you have it. A little bit of wisdom garnered after years of research and study at the School of Hard Knocks. It's time-tested stuff, guaranteed to save you much unhappiness, anguish, heartache—and maybe the love of your family and your entire fortune to boot. Not a bad deal for the price of this book, eh?

Make all the relationships you want, move in and out of each other's houses at will, take weekend trips with lovers and defiantly register in hotels as an unmarried couple, join the in people in the first decade of the 21st century and live it up. Do as you please for once and hang the consequences.

Remember, this could very easily be your last decade so don't blow it.

Survival Rules
1. Don't marry again after sixty!
2. Beware of gold diggers.
3. Old people are set in their ways—and so are you.
4. Your kids will be pissed if you marry again and with good reason.
5. Don't end up an involuntary nurse.
6. Live together in sin.
7. We live in the 21st century; there are no rules anymore.
8. Remember, always practice safe sex.

CHAPTER EIGHT

Voting

As a quick follow-up to the preceding chapter, which ends with an admonition to make a practice of dumping incumbents, let me briefly expound on politicians and politics.

Politics is a scurvy business, a business that attracts scurvy people. With rare exceptions all politicians are amoral scoundrels whose chief concerns are centered on stealing, graft, bribery, kickbacks, junkets, and staying in office. They have no other interests.

We all know what politics is about, of course. It's the art of making deals, of compromise and quid pro quos. The deals made have to do with the interests of chief concern to politicians (see above.) The interests of the people, our interests, are never allowed to interfere with the interests of the politicians.

What does this mean to you? It means you must look out for yourself insofar as that's possible. The inimitable Mark Twain in Puddin' Head Wilson wrote, "Tell me where a man gits his cornpone an' I'll tell you where he gits his 'pinions." Always vote your cornpone. Vote your interests. Vote your pocketbook. Always.

If you're a pensioner without health insurance, demand national health care. Vote for it. Support people who support such a program. Is Social Security insufficient? Raise it. Threaten your congressman if he won't go along.

The point is everybody else is doing the same and they always have. Join the AARP and lobby for your interests just as the oil people, farmers, and defense contractors do. Beyond this, avoid politics. Refuse to run for office yourself if you value your reputation, your very soul. And don't encourage others to run, either. Only harm will come from such activity.

Your only defense against these jackals is to limit their time at the carcass. Strike terror into their hearts. Demand term limits in all elections everywhere. Refuse to amend the Constitution so Arnold can run for president. Insist that these four-flushers get honest work after six or eight years of abusing the citizenry and lining their pockets. Wipe the smirks from their pasty faces and let them know they're dealing with enlightened people now, people who will no longer allow themselves to be victims of brazen theft and fraud and the conniving of cheap crooks.

Survival Rules
1. Politics is a dirty game; refuse to play.
2. Don't associate with politicians or be seen in their company.
3. Imprison as many of them as you can catch.
4. Limit their terms.
5. Always vote your cornpone.

CHAPTER NINE

Old-timers and Crime

If you're an old-timer in America and happen to live in or very near a large city, you'll have to be especially careful in terms of your personal safety. While overall crime is down these days, there's still a surfeit of thugs and hoodlums to make things hot for the elderly among us. Crooks and muggers and second-story men like to target old people because they're often helpless and easy prey. It's up to you to protect yourself, as you know you can't rely on anybody else to do it.

Obviously, you need a plan, some scheme to deal with crime in your home and street that will enable you to outwit the thieves and murderers through decisive action of your own. I have such a plan.

You can start with solid home security. Install good locks on all doors and buy the best. Get the kind of doors that stop bullets, thick ones with armor plate built in. Put in deadbolts, too. And get some chains for your doors in case anybody gets past the locks and deadbolts.

Secure all windows with standard window locks and put sticks in the tracks of all sliding windows and doors. Drill holes through the window frame and into the sides and stick nails in them so the windows can't be jimmied. Do the same for second-story windows since most burglars can climb like monkeys and will probe your upstairs defenses at will.

A burglar alarm is a good idea, too. Get one that emits an ear-splitting scream when it goes off. You want to be damn sure your neighbors are inconvenienced enough that they'll do something when your alarm sounds. You can add one of those medic alert gadgets that let you tell people when you've fallen and can't get up. They can send the EMS people out and maybe they'll scare the burglars away.

Or start a neighborhood watch program. Set up a headquarters to synchronize your movements. Hold regular meetings and invite guest speakers to bolster flagging morale. Have everybody turn on their outside lights and consider chipping in to install searchlights every six or seven houses to throw even more light on the subject. Have everybody get those motion detector lights that come on whenever someone approaches within a few feet of the house.

Send out car patrols. Or even foot patrols if you have neighbors who are spry enough to actually walk around the neighborhood. Report any suspicious sign, any character who meets the profile of your average burglar or mugger, i.e., anybody who's a stranger in the area. Set up ambushes and try to catch muggers in the act. Be creative.

In addition to the above, it's a good idea to learn the basics of self-defense so you can handle yourself in hand-to-hand combat should you ever be taken by surprise. A few lessons from the nearest karate school will prove invaluable.

Now some of these places offer a kind of watered-down course aimed at senior citizens and small children, but you don't want that one unless you plan on being attacked only by senior citizens and small children. Since you're more likely to be assaulted by some muscle-bound two-hundred-pound galoot wielding a ball bat or butcher knife, you want lessons in how to deal with such types.

Anyway, sign up for karate lessons and learn how to smash piles of bricks to smithereens with either hand. Practice kicking peoples' heads off from a standing start and learn how to fall from great heights and land without breaking anything you really need. Get yourself one of those karate suits and wear a headband. Have your picture taken in your new regalia and show it to all your friends to let them know you're nobody to fool with, by God!

Get a karate school decal for your car bumper and wear a karate patch on your jacket so crooks will know you're a trained professional. Carry stuff in a gym bag instead of a regular shopping bag and muggers will think you're on your way home from the gym and avoid you. Stand tall when you walk and move with determination and a sense of purpose and dupe them into believing you're a person with a goal, a man on his way someplace.

I know it may be hard to pull this last dodge off if you're using a cane or one of those walkers for locomotion or your spine is curved like a shepherd's crook from advanced osteoporosis and your top speed is a less than brisk shuffle, but do what you can. It's all a matter of image, of your appearance of vulnerability. It's the nine-pound cat puffing himself up to look like a small lion in an effort to scare off the mastiff that's closing in on him. If it works for the cat, it can work for you.

Okay, so some of you are saying, "Are you nuts, for God's sake? I'm eighty-eight years old and you expect me to learn karate and fight two-hundred-pound burglars? And what's this falling from great heights without getting hurt crap? I fell off my chair last year and broke a hip, I did, so how in hell am I gonna fall from great heights and...?"

All right, these are good points and I anticipated them. Sure, there are certain drawbacks to some of the above suggestions, but most of them will prove useful for most of you. There are, however, certain other things you may do to survive in one of America's large cities in the 21st century, and one of them is to arm yourself to the teeth.

Muggers and burglars and similar types are armed, aren't they? Aren't these guys notorious for carrying guns and knives? When the mugger confronts you on the street, doesn't he punctuate his demands with an enormous pistol?

Incidentally, all guns can be described as enormous regardless of their actual size. When the victim is questioned he describes a gun with a foot-wide barrel even if it turns out the robber used an air pistol.

Why should the crooks be the only ones with arms? Isn't arming for self-protection a tradition in this country? In fact, I think there's even something in the Constitution about this unless I'm mistaken—or if those assholes on the Supreme Court haven't excised it entirely by this time.

Anyway, for real protection from the criminal element in modern-day America, get yourself a gun and learn how to use it. Even the Democrats gave up their fight against guns and now encourage everybody to have one.

It's not hard, really. Anybody can buy a gun nowadays, as there are gun shops in our better neighborhoods all across this great land and any sap can stroll in and order up a nifty automatic sixteen-shot 9mm pistol complete with pearl-handled grip and a racing stripe. The following scenario might well be re-enacted by you in your own friendly neighborhood gun shop.

"I'd like to see something in a nice gun," you tell the man lounging behind the counter, "something stylish and not too unwieldy."

"Sure thing," he says, hooking his thumbs in his cartridge belt. "We have guns for every purpose and to fit every pocketbook. What did you want the gun for?"

"Well," you say, somewhat taken aback, "to shoot people, I guess. What else are guns for?"

"Oh, you want a gun for protection then?"

"Yes, that's right, a gun for protection."

"Okay, now we're getting somewhere," he says. "Here's a nice little number that's very popular, a .38 special revolver with good stopping power."

"Stopping power?"

"Sure," he beams at you. "When this baby hits a

guy it'll stop him cold. You do want to stop him cold, don't you?"

"Of course," you say, not sure what that means. What you'd really hoped for was a gun that'd stop a guy dead, but maybe cold would do as well.

"Then this is the gun for you," he says. "And only four-hundred bucks."

"Okay, I'll take it," you say, reaching for your credit card.

"Now, how about your backup?"

"My what?"

"Backup. You need a backup gun in case somebody gets away with your main piece. Here, this one is a dandy. See, it's small and can easily be hidden in your sock like this. Now, suppose somebody gets the drop on you and takes your .38 away. Okay, as soon as he looks away you bend down and come up with your backup gun and bam! You stop him cold!"

He beams at you again, obviously pleased with his scheme, and you are impressed, indeed.

"Say," you say, "that is clever. I'll take the little one, too."

"Good. That's two-and-a-quarter. And you'll want a shotgun for your home, too."

"I will?"

"Of course. Everybody knows the best weapon for the home is a shotgun. Why, hell, you can't miss with one of these babies. I sold a 16-gauge shotgun to a seventy-eight-year-old lady and she cleaned a whole nest of burglars out of her attic the first week she had it. Here, take a look at this double-barrel with a modified choke, it's just the thing for winging burglars."

You take the gun and sweep it around the room while drilling imaginary crooks on the fly and have to admit it has a nice heft to it. What the hell, if you're doing something, do it right.

"Okay, I'll take the shotgun, too," you say.

You pick up several hundred rounds of ammo and a case of shotgun shells, a gun cleaning kit, a couple of holsters, and a .30 caliber deer rifle with a 'scope for picking off burglars at long range, and the owner genially invites you down into the basement to see his gun range.

You open the door and are greeted by a steady staccato of gun fire, which fills the air and reverberates around the room while acrid clouds of burned gunpowder gather in the atmosphere. It's a scene to warm the heart of the most dedicated National Rifle Ass'n member and fledgling psychotic, and one that warms your own heart as you conjure up visions of the surprise you'll have for the next mugger you meet.

You join a bunch of guys on the firing line and observe that they all wear small American flag patches and tattoos on their forearms saying things like Death Before Dishonor and Mother. You spend the next several hours test-firing your new guns, practicing hand grenade throwing, and learning the intricacies of bayonet fighting. By the time you leave the place you know you're ready to repel a full-scale invasion by Attila the Hun.

And that's it. Now you can meet the crooks on their own terms. Carry your guns everywhere. Never let them take you unawares. Always sit with your back against the wall in public places like restaurants and bars as this will enable you to keep an eye on any would-be assassins who might sneak up on you. It will also provide you with an air of mystery and intrigue among friends who notice your penchant for wall-based seating.

Stroll boldly along foggy waterfronts on moonless nights hoping, like Clint Eastwood in the movie, that somebody will make your day. Move fearlessly through deserted streets, routinely make eye contact with homeless people and stare them down secure in the thought that you're armed to the teeth and can shoot them dead if they make a false move.

What about a gun license, you ask? Aren't there laws against carrying concealed weapons on city streets? What if the police catch you with a gun? Will you go to jail?

Certainly not. Remember, you're an old-timer, a senior citizen who's earned a hallowed place in society and the respect of others. What judge wants to raise the ire of his constituents by sentencing some octogenarian to jail for merely carrying a gun for personal protection, especially in a lawless society that is admittedly unable to provide this venerable duffer with said protection?

Besides, suppose you do shoot some mugger who's threatening to smash your skull in with a brick and the cops arrest you and charge you with manslaughter or something. So what? Would you rather not have the gun and end up with a smashed skull when this nut raps you with his brick? On the one hand you risk jail while on the other you risk a smashed skull. So?

Anyway, if you do get arrested just throw yourself on the mercy of the court. Point out that you're an orphan, you fought bravely for your country in one or another of its various wars, and you just made a generous contribution to the judge's re-election campaign.

What's that? You say one of your parents is still living, you never were in the army, and you didn't make that contribution? Say, what is this? Are you paying attention here? Who gives a damn whether any of this stuff is true? We're trying to keep you out of the big house, for God's sake. We're lying. What difference does it make? Tell the old fool whatever he wants to hear. After all, he's used to lying, isn't he? How do you think he became a judge in the first place?

Enlist the aid of the press. Demand the AARP people be alerted. Send out an appeal for contributions to your defense fund. Wear threadbare clothes and feign great infirmities. Tremble a lot. Pop breath mints and hint they're nitroglycerin pills for your heart. Lay it on thick enough and no jury in the world would ever convict you of anything much less for shooting a thug armed with a brick.

Remember, old-timers can do whatever the hell they want. Well, in this case you wanted to shoot a mugger and you did.

End of discussion.

As you can see, it is possible to live in a crime-infested American city in the 21st century if you will assert yourself and take charge of your own destiny. Millions of our senior citizens are doing just that and you can be one of them if you'll only will it so.

Survival Rules
1. Don't rely on the cops; only you can protect you.
2. Get home security including armor plate, alarms, vicious dogs, spotlights, electrified fences, etc.
3. Start a neighborhood watch program. Enlist all known busybodies.
4. Put up a bold front. Stare homeless people down, sneer at Crips and Bloods alike. Refuse to be intimidated.
5. Sign up for karate lessons.
6. Get a gun. Better still, get two guns and learn how to use them.

CHAPTER TEN

Children/Grandchildren

Like the poor you will always have your children with you. Oh, they may live in another state or even on another continent but they'll be a part of your life to the very end. You can't get rid of them no matter what you do.

It can help if you move to a distant city somewhere and make yourself as inaccessible as possible. At least then you wouldn't actually have to deal with them physically on a day-to-day basis. One guy I knew encouraged his kids to move to California because he planned to retire out there and they could all be together, etc. Then he retired to Florida and hardly ever saw any of them again.

Now, don't misunderstand me. I'm not suggesting that your kids aren't okay—but there are people out there whose kids drive them nuts and bring nothing but heartbreak and grief into their lives and I pen these lines for their benefit.

For example, most people's kids need financial help, a lesson most Boomers have learned by heart. They lose their jobs and end up on relief and guess whom they turn to? Imagine this scenario. You're home tying some new fishing flies and planning that week in Idaho fishing those excellent trout streams when the phone rings.

"Uh, Dad? Yeah, it's me. I got some bad news. They're not buildin' that new plant, after all. Moved it lock, stock 'n barrel to Mexico. But you don't have to worry 'bout us. We're doin' okay. Sally got a job in a sweatshop and the Salvation Army's got a place for us. They got some Haitians livin' in some substandard housing and the government says they have to move them to better quarters. Just as soon as they move out we can move right in and..."

What can you do? You sigh mightily and put your flies away along with any thought of that fishing trip. The money goes to the kid.

Nonsense, some will say. Why give up your fishing trip for the kid? You've worked hard all your life and earned some peace and quiet in your old age. Isn't the kid on his own now? Are you still responsible for him? Why not just tell him to let you know his new address when he gets settled and make those reservations?

Because you can't, that's why. You're stuck. Your kid needs help and you're the only one who can help him. It's not rational or fair, there's no law that requires it, you're not even bound morally or ethically, but you still have to help him. Ask any parent.

If they're nearby you spend all your time refereeing their marital spats. Daughter is pissed because her husband's carrying on with some bimbo down at the office and you never hear the end of it. She's talking divorce and lawyers and lengthy court trials and would you keep the kids for three months while she establishes residence in Reno or some such place and on and on.

What really terrifies you, though, is the fear that

daughter will go through with the divorce and move back home with the kids—"home" being your house, of course. If this happens you'll end up raising a second batch of kids while your daughter reorganizes her life, a process that could take anywhere from months to many years.

What's even worse, you could have two or more daughters and end up with enough kids to launch a good-sized orphanage. Isn't that a cheery thought for the average elderly parent who's already sacrificed one complete lifetime under the oppressive yoke of parenthood? The people who claim kids are cheaper by the dozen are fools or nuts or both—and I don't mean just in terms of money.

Can you order them off your doorstep when daughter and kids show up on your porch during a raging blizzard and ask for shelter? Of course not. You invite them in and do your duty as a parent. Cancel all prior plans, abandon lifelong dreams, give yourself over to their needs. Your life is now their life; you'll live for them.

Can't happen to you, you say? Do you know there are millions of grandparents who are raising their grandkids even now? These are old-timers like you, people who served their time and earned a complete pardon from parenthood. They were once carefree and happy and entertained visions of retirement with lots of golf and bridge and restful summer afternoons; instead, they're raising daughter's kids and wondering where they went wrong.

And it's not fair, either. It's a given that your own

children will bedevil you until Grim shows up and calls your number, but it should end there. Nobody should be asked to go through such traumatic events a second time, especially not when they're old folks with lowered immune systems and a tendency to fall and break hips and miscellaneous other bones on a regular basis.

It can't be helped, though, for children truly are a life sentence. If a child of yours scores a remarkable triumph and cops a Pulitzer Prize you'll share in it because you're his parent. But if that same child is sent to the big house for his third armed robbery rap you'll share that cell with him until parole releases the pair of you. You'll rejoice when he does and hurt when he hurts. His misfortunes will be yours along with his victories.

For having children is a gamble at best, a throw of the dice with Dame Fortune as the house. Lots of people crap out. Others eventually make their point but always the hard way. Still others roll a winner and scoop up their winnings with wide grins on their mugs. It's all a part of some vast karma, some force or energy that directs our affairs in ways too mysterious even for a god to follow.

But all this is too late for you, isn't it? You've long since had your kids and they've bedeviled you and grown up and moved out and left you on your own at last. You've paid your dues and then some, you're home free—or should be, anyway.

Then your kids had kids of their own, your grandchildren, and turned you into a grandparent whether you liked it or not. And this isn't all bad, you know, as grandchildren are different from your own kids in that you aren't solely responsible for raising them. In fact, playing with the grandkids for an afternoon and then handing them back over to their mothers while you go take a nap is one of the joys of being a grandparent.

Insofar as this works, it's not a bad deal. But have a care. Your kids will be tempted to enlist Granny as a built-in babysitter and exploit her to the full extent of the law. You'll find yourself on call seven nights a week and every weekend. Daughter will drop her kids off at Granny's on the slightest whim if you let her.

The secret is don't let her.

Tell them straight out that you love your grandkids more than life itself but you refuse to be exploited. No babysitting without advance notice and complete concurrence on your part. Be firm. Desperate parents can detect weakness and indecision clear across town. It's all just a matter of laying down the ground rules early on and then sticking to them to the bitter end.

However, all this said, we have a single grandchild, a most remarkable seven-year-old little girl named Emily who came all the way from China to live with my son and his wife. She's bright and funny and charming; we love her visits, spoil her with gifts on the slightest pretext, cheerfully contribute to her college fund, and know we're lucky to have her in our lives.

Lots of grandparents are as lucky as we are. I hope you're one of them.

Survival Rules
1. You've raised your kids; don't raise anybody else's if you can help it. (Some of you won't be able to help it.)
2. Refuse to become an unpaid babysitter for your grandkids.
3. Expect to serve as your kids' personal banker until Grim closes out your account.
4. On the other hand, there are a lot of Emilys out there.

CHAPTER ELEVEN

Second Careers

People have the notion that life ends somewhere around fifty or sixty and everything's downhill after that. So-called old people are supposed to act their age and gracefully fade away into the gathering dusk with a minimum of fuss and noise.

Haven't they had their chance? Shouldn't they make room for younger people who are waiting for their own chance in life? Doesn't retirement mean you're supposed to get the hell out of the way and clear a path for the new generation?

Nonsense. You're not dead yet. Oh, you may not be operating on all cylinders anymore, you may be a step slower than before and not able to jump quite as high, but that doesn't mean you can't run or jump at all. The race isn't over until Grim flags you down and rounds you up. Until that fateful moment, you are alive and have a right to be.

You've put in your thirty-year sentence teaching school or selling widgets or building cars and now you're retired and free to do anything you like. If you're like most of us you probably aren't living the life of Riley and could use some extra income for frivolous things like bread and housing. Okay, so launch a second career.

Everybody's doing it. The land is swarming with old-timers busily engaged in new enterprises of every imaginable kind. Old people take classes in colleges and even earn degrees in their eighties. They open businesses and lay the foundations for empires.

Take Col. Sanders and his chicken business, for example. This old guy took his first Social Security check at sixty-five and hit the road to peddle his new chicken recipe. In no time his Kentucky Fried Chicken business grew into a national chain and made him a multi-millionaire and all this happened after he "retired."

Am I suggesting you start a national chicken restaurant chain then? Of course not. Some of you may not even like chicken. The point is there are probably things that interest you, things you never had time for when you were working.

Maybe you're an amateur photographer and know a lot about cameras and how they work. Okay, take freelance pictures for the media. Hire on with a local newspaper. Offer to work for nothing until you can show you do good work. Submit photos to contests. Frame your best ones and hold a one-man show at a neighborhood tavern. You could be the next Ansel Adams or Annie Leibovitz.

In other words, now's your chance to do something you really like to do. You've always liked photography so become a photographer. Who says you can't do it? What's stopping you? Do you realize that once you declare to the world that you are a photographer and begin taking pictures of things you'll actually be a photographer?

That's all it takes.

But suppose you don't like chicken and know

nothing about photography. Then what? Do something else. You like the theatre? Join a community theatre group. Insist that they stage lots of plays with roles for octogenarians and demand to play the lead. Offer to direct. Or even write a play. Who knows? You may turn out to be the Grandma Moses of Broadway.

Or do outlandish things. Who will gainsay an old-timer doing whatever he wants to do? Become a critic and review skin shows in your town. Frequent all the topless bars and write a column about the performers. If you include pictures you can assure your success.

Take up painting and wear a beret. Learn the jargon and hang around coffeehouses talking with real artists. Smoke thin cigars and splatter your shirt with paint to add to the illusion. Splash paint around like Jackson Pollock and call it art. Attend gallery exhibitions and drink up all their free Chablis.

What's that? You say you can't draw a straight line? So what? Tell them you're a modern artist and you won't have to know diddly about real art. Such knowledge or skill isn't required of modern artists. You just get some canvas or even an old sheet and make some markings on the damn thing. Use a coffee can lid for perfect circles. Paint in some daubs of color at randomly selected spots and flick more paint here and there and you'll have a perfectly acceptable "painting" that will fool even the most astute art experts in the business.

Some will say your painting's no good? What the hell do they know? These same jokers said Van Gogh couldn't paint, either. Who's to say your stuff won't be hanging in the Metropolitan some day?

Or even better, you can become an art thief. Case the local art museum. These places are easy targets. Slip in and make off with a Picasso or a couple of Hoppers. Hand them out of a window to an accomplice waiting below. Stick with smaller pictures so you won't stand out as you steal the stuff. It's hard to be inconspicuous if you move about a museum with a 6X8 foot portrait of Blue Boy on your shoulder.

You can hold the pictures for ransom and earn that extra money you need to supplement your inadequate pension. Call the press and demand that the art critic serve as a go-between. Think of all the fun you can have negotiating the return of the artwork for cash and a promise of immunity.

You'll make news in every country on the planet and be an instantaneous celebrity. Talk show hosts will call and send a limo to carry your venerable carcass to their shows. Politicians will rally to your cause, Hollywood will buy your life story, pretty girls/handsome men will throw themselves at your feet. How's that for adding a little spice to the average old-timer's otherwise dreary life?

You say you might get caught and sent to jail? Don't be silly; you're forgetting whom you are. Nobody sends octogenarians to jail. Suppose the worst-case scenario.

You're stealing Hopper's Nighthawks and the guard catches you red-handed and he calls the cops. They arrive and find an old geezer with a walker and nearly blinded by cataracts the size of dimes.

"Where's the crook?" the cop asks on entering.

"That's him there," the guard says.

"What?" the cop says. "This is the guy?"

"Be careful!" the guard says warily. "You can never tell what these old guys are thinking. He might pull a knife on you."

"Are you nuts?" the cop says. "This guy's a hundred years old, for God's sake. He couldn't even pick up Hopper's Nighthawks let alone steal the damn thing."

"Oh, yeah?" the guard says. "I caught the old fraud in the act. He was handing it out the window to another old guy below in a wheelchair. We almost caught him, too, but he was too fast for us. He dropped the picture, though, because he needed both hands to work the wheelchair."

"What the hell am I supposed to do with this guy?" the cop demands. "If I bring him in I'll be the laughingstock of the entire force. We don't even have any place to put guys who are a hundred years old."

They'll take you downtown and book you for art theft. You cagily hint that you're part of an international art theft ring that's stolen hundreds of millions of dollars in art from museums around the world and the press will flock like rats around an abattoir. They'll have a field day complete with pictures and interviews and your name will be a household word almost overnight.

And your trial? More hoopla. Claim you were living on dog food and announce that you only stole to eat. Blame Congress and whoever happens to be president at the time and denounce a society that forces its old people to become thieves. Insist that you be tried by your peers and stack the jury with other old duffers who know what it's like to be old and will lend a sympathetic ear.

They'll never convict you. The judge will be embarrassed, the nation ashamed. Old-timers everywhere will rise to your defense and demand you be declared innocent. You'll be turned loose with a great fanfare and paraded down Main Street with a brass band and a lot of scantily clad dancing girls.

See what you can have if you'll just go for it?

Why, there's no end to the number and wonder of things you can do as a member of the geriatric set. Start a lonely-hearts club for people over, say, seventy-five. Match up widows and widowers. Pair off divorcees/widows with their male counterparts. If there are any old bat virgin librarians around, fix them up with anyone not yet dead and you'll bring much joy into the librarians' lives. I'm not sure what you'll be bringing into the lives of the not dead yet partners but, what the hell, you only do what you can.

By the way, you charge them for the service, of course. Who knows? You may be able to sell franchises and situate branches in every retirement condo and old folks' home in the country. A word of caution, though, no long term deals. These people are old, remember, and likely to keel over dead as mackerels at any moment. Keep all deals short. Get all money up front. They say they'll pay next month but will they still be around then?

Do you see how limitless your opportunities are? Why, the years from sixty-to-ninety are wonderful years, some of the best you've ever known, if you only see them for what they are and take advantage of them.

Get out there and do something. Take tap-dancing lessons and try for a stage career. Bill yourself as the world's oldest amateur tap dancer and turn pro on them. Learn to ski. Become a cardsharp and frequent card rooms in Vegas. Learn to fly and claim age discrimination when the airlines refuse to hire you as a pilot.

Get a penile implant and join the swingers. Rent a monkey and an organ grinder's outfit and go into business for yourself. Look for a chance to open monkey franchises across America. Hang around the track and work to turn into a colorful character out of Damon Runyon.

March to a different drummer, for God's sake. Time's running out on you, Grim's gaining on you by leaps and bounds. What are you waiting for? If not now, when?

What have you got to lose?

Survival Rules
   1. Launch a second career and pick something that's fun this time around.
   2. Do outlandish things. (See Freedom chapter.)
   3. Join a community theatre and demand to play the lead.
   4. Tell people you're an artist and hang around

galleries.
5. Or become an art thief and appear on all the talk shows.
6. Remember the Colonel. If he can do it, why not you?

CHAPTER TWELVE

Money/Investments

It's a good idea to keep a close eye on your ready cash as a general rule, but it's an even better idea when you sail past sixty-two and into advanced old age. Remember, you're a Boomer and don't have the fancy pensions and golden parachutes that your parents received. Usually, whatever a person has at retirement is pretty much what he's going to end up with and that makes it imperative that he not do anything stupid and lose some or all of his assets.

A man in his thirties or forties still has time to recoup his losses if he makes a bad deal but a guy eighty or so would be hard pressed to save anything for an old age that was already upon him. Even if he got a job and saved like mad he'd probably run out of time before he could acquire enough to mean anything.

So when you retire it's a good idea to have your money in sound investments that will be there when you want them. First, let's look at some of the investments you should avoid on the grounds that they're either too risky for a retired person or because they're outright frauds run by guys using pay phones in the state pen.

Beware of all mining stocks, especially when the guy selling them wears a thin moustache and talks real fast. The more exotic they are the more likely they are to be scams. Gold mines are no good. Platinum and silver mines are as bad and uranium mines are worse.

The same goes for gemstones. Diamond mine stock is great if your name is de Beers. You should also pass on ruby, sapphire, and emerald mine stocks.

They sell this stuff to farmers and village halfwits who are impressed with the thought of owning jewels. In fact, a lot of them buy the actual stones and lock them away in safe deposit boxes in hopes they'll grow in value and make the owner rich. The stones always come elaborately packaged and are invariably worth only a fraction of what they paid for them.

Besides, it's too tricky to buy these things unless you know a lot about precious stones. The things come in all sizes, shapes, and weights with varying planes of symmetry, clarity, and iridescence. What looks like a magnificent emerald to the average farmer is easily recognized as a flawed paste copy by anyone knowledgeable in the trade—always a seller, of course.

So skip the exotic stones and phony gold stocks.

Watch out for guys offering to double your money in a few weeks, too. More people lose the farm by falling for the old 30% interest guarantee than through any other scam. Not a day goes by but that you read where people have been wiped out by the failure of some phony mortgage company or broker who turned out to be running some Ponzi scheme or other.

When you get into their story, though, you find out they were getting 25% interest when everybody else was paying 6%. These people were drawn in by their own greed and happily cashed dividend checks and scoffed at their more cautious neighbors until the roof fell in and they were cleaned out.

What'd they expect? Nobody pays 25% or 30% interest when the going rate is 6%. Don't people know that? Investments that pay these high returns are almost always frauds and should be avoided at all costs. There's always a catch. Wouldn't you think anybody who'd lived to be eighty or so would have finally learned that?

The truth is you should probably avoid the stock market altogether. Buying and selling individual stocks is a game for the pros and not for retired farmers and erstwhile schoolteachers. You're better off if you stick to good mutual funds where they spread the risk and minimize any potential losses. Or, even better, invest in an index fund that's based on the entire market or the S&P 500 fund or something similar. (See the Vanguard people.) Any broker can steer you into some good funds and you don't even need a broker for an index fund.

In any case, remember the '90s and all those dot.com outfits. People started a shop in a garage and a year later sold out for billions but guys like you went broke when the market went south. It will happen again.

But there's another caveat. Brokers. Investment counselors. Money managers. Financial advisers. Insurance guys. Even bankers. All of them are out to skin old-timers like you. They rub their hands in eager anticipation when they see you coming in with your walker and a glazed look in your eyes. You're manna from heaven to these guys. They know you haven't the foggiest notion of how to handle money and will believe anything that's told you with conviction and seeming sincerity.

They'll spring from their chairs and tenderly help you to get seated and comfortable. Fawning is their trademark. They'll even have an aide take your walker out and give it a good polishing. They'll claim you remind them of their own dearly departed grandparents and listen with rapt attention to your long-winded stories of life back in Iowa or wherever.

In short, they'll work to become your friend, someone you can trust. They'll find out what church you attend and claim to be charter members. If you're a Bible thumper, they'll thump, too. Let them know you're a Republican and, by God, so are they. By the time they get done with the average octogenarian they've convinced him that they're the straightest shooting, highest principled, most trustworthy dude in the entire financial world. Next thing you know they've got carte blanche access to the old duffer's bank account and in no time they've churned him into bankruptcy or worse.

The point is you can't trust these guys. They make money by doing mysterious things with yours, things so mysterious that Blackstone himself couldn't adequately explain what the hell happened to your dough. Remember the cardinal rule: You can trust no one with your money!

If you do get somebody to advise you, check him out on a regular basis. Insist on frequent audits by a crackerjack CPA outfit. Demand that he be bonded.

Make sure he carries malpractice insurance. Hint that you have friends in the mob and imply they'll be pissed if anyone abuses you. Relate the story of how your uncle was fleeced by his broker and the enraged uncle threw said broker from his thirtieth-story window in a fit of pique.

Get his Social Security number, find out where he lives and what schools his kids attend, and send his prints to the F.B.I. to see if the clown is wanted anywhere. Only after all this should you agree to let him get his lunch hooks on any part of your ready cash. Even so, you'll still probably have to sue the crooked bastard to recover what he steals from you.

You can find a financial adviser by asking friends to recommend someone they're using, but have a care. First make sure they still have some of their own money left to indicate their own success with this joker. If they're broke and facing eviction from the family farm you may want to look further for a financial adviser.

In general, stick your cash in the aforementioned mutual funds and maybe some government bonds or CDs or IRAs and refuse to do business with anybody selling anything else. You may not make a killing in the market, but you won't likely be killed, either.

What about loans to relatives and friends, people who need help and have nowhere else to turn? Are you nuts? Tell these guys you're not a bank. If banks won't lend them money, why in hell would you want to?

These four-flushers are poor credit risks or they could get bank loans like everybody else. Do you think bankers are stupid? They won't lend people money unless they're damn sure they're going to get it back with interest. Your worthless cousin has a record like Jesse James' scratchpad and he wants you to lend him money?

If you do give him any money, stop around to your doctor and sign up for a brain scan to see which part of yours has gone on the blink. It'll probably be the frontal lobe that houses whatever supply of good sense you have left.

Do you lend money to your children? We've already answered this one, haven't we? You will but you probably shouldn't. And when you do, consider it a gift and not a loan because it's highly unlikely you'll ever see it again, anyway.

Oh, go ahead and sign a note with the particulars spelled out in detail to set a legal tone to the whole business even though you know the ingrates have no intention of paying it back. Everybody'll feel better if they go along with the fiction that this is a bona fide legal contract, which they fully intend to fulfill in its entirety. What's the difference as long as everybody knows what's really going on?

So there you have it, a primer on safe and sane money management for old-timers. You've worked hard and managed to save a little for your declining years. Now it's up to you to see that you don't do anything stupid and end up a ward of the state because some two-bit shyster has shorn you like somebody's little lost lamb.

Unbelievable.

Survival Rules
1. Trust no one!
2. Submit your broker's fingerprints to the FBI to see if he's wanted anywhere.
3. Avoid guys who wear thin moustaches and talk real fast.
4. Resist all schemes offering to double your money in a hurry.
5. Trust no one!
6. Stay with mutual funds and away from the market unless you know what the hell you're doing.
7. Don't lend money to friends or relatives; send them to a bank.
8. Trust no one!

CHAPTER THIRTEEN

Dressing Right

You'll remember that we've already seen where old people have the freedom to do anything they damn well please because they are old and no longer accountable for their conduct. This applies to how they dress and maintain their personal appearance. There are two perspectives to consider in sartorial matters and each is a viable option for you.

The first approach is a casual one. You've spent thirty or more years wearing Brooks Brothers suits and wing-tip shoes while toiling for IBM or some stuffy bank and now you're an old geezer who doesn't work for anybody. You're tired of looking like William F. Buckley? So don't.

Lose the suit and shoes. Get yourself a jogging suit and some of those ubiquitous white gym shoes everybody's wearing nowadays. Tie a red bandana around your forehead if you feel like it. Wear an earring. Consider getting a tattoo, one with a snake entwined around a dagger. Affect dark sunglasses, even indoors

Do whatever you want. Send a snapshot of yourself outfitted as outlined above to the IBM people and demand to know what they intend to do about it, by God.

I know men who've been retired for a decade and have never worn a tie since their retirement party. Some of them don't even own a suit. These guys think they're dressed up when they put on a pair of pressed khakis with their sneakers. And who's to gainsay them at this stage?

Same for women, of course. They can and do dress like the men. Casual is the byword. Shorts and sneakers and pants are considered chic in retirement communities from coast to coast. Of course, sensible shoes are a must for people using walkers and/or canes. Few old ladies are willing to don spiked heels no matter how good the damn things make their legs look.

Again, some caveats, though.

Keep an eye on the little things. Look out for gravy stains on your shirtfront. Check that jacket. Are those mustard stains on the sleeve? Does your collar look like a much-used antimacassar? What about missing buttons? Is your sweater buttoned crookedly?

A lot of old-timers allow themselves to go to seed once they retire. For one thing, their eyes go south on them and they just can't see gravy stains anymore. As a result they end up wearing a vest that looks like a well-used napkin streaked and spotted with the residue of varicolored sauces. People with good vision see these stains, though, and they'll write you down as an old-timer who's slipping swiftly into senility.

So inspect those clothes. Hold them up to a good light and scrutinize them carefully. If necessary, enlist the aid of somebody who can see. Even a small child will do. The little tyke will see pinhead-sized spots clear across the room and can point them out to you. Remember, it's okay to go the casual route as you drift into your dotage but at least try to make the trip with a clean shirt.

In fact, it's generally a good idea to play down the casual stuff and that leads to your second option. You might want to pay even more attention to your appearance than is strictly required as a retiree. It's possible to maintain a certain well-bred look even after age has overtaken you and ravaged you from stem to stern. I'll go even further and recommend it.

Consider. It's already bad enough just turning into an old duffer without heaping additional burdens on yourself. People regard old-timers as nuisances as it is and give them short shrift whenever they can. They relegate them to a solitary existence in dingy two-room apartments in parts of town no longer considered safe. Millions are shoveled into the homes of unwilling relatives where they're abused and have their Social Security checks stolen. Others are dispatched to nursing homes and convalescent centers and the odd hospice to await the arrival of Grim and his printouts.

But if you've noticed these victims are always people who look and act like really old people. They're usually wearing mismatched shoes and the omnipresent food-splattered clothing mentioned above. Most of them need haircuts and manicures and a lot of them could use a good bath. They're rounded up and shipped away because they're unsightly. People don't like to look at them because they remind them of their own precarious grip on sanity and normalcy.

So fool them. Dress spiffily. Shine your shoes and wear clean socks. Don a sport coat of an evening and some real pants with a crease in them. Ladies can get their hair done every week and wear makeup and put on a dress in lieu of those jogging suits. They can get manicures and facials and designer glasses. In other words, let the world know from your appearance that you're not dead yet.

You'll notice a remarkable change in how people treat you right from the start. An old guy in dirty chinos and a scruffy beard is regarded as a loser, somebody to be avoided. But put the same old guy in a classy outfit and give him a look of prosperity and suddenly he's a man of parts, a man of consequence, a man entitled to respect and even deference.

Try it for yourself. Dress in your usual scruffy style and stop by a new car showroom to browse. The salesmen see an old fogy kicking tires and they mark him down as a loser who couldn't possibly afford a new car and they go on cleaning their nails and ogling the secretary with the big hooters.

So go away and come back the next day in a suit and tie. Saunter in and start browsing. This time the salesmen look up and see an affluent-looking dude in a suit and clean shirt and now they see an older gentleman who's obviously a man of some means and they tear their eyes from the hooters and hurry over to wait on you. It works every time.

It's true. We're superficial. We buy whatever we see. Dress like a millionaire and we'll take your word for it. Look like a bum and that's what you'll be.

The same goes for our mental outlook. So you're old. So what? Don't forget, the only alternative to age is an early spot on Grim's printouts. Who wouldn't rather be old? If it's truly good to be alive, then act like it.

Put a bounce in your step, if you can walk at all. Straighten up, if that's possible. Women with a bad case of dowager's hump should compensate by pretending they're looking for something they just dropped. Assume a jaunty air. Look people straight in the eye and let them know they're dealing with a real man and/or woman. People will treat you as a real person if you can trick them into thinking you are one.

By the way, dressing up is a real boon for all you guys out there who still dream of being sweetly dangerous among the women, as Cyrano once remarked. Surely you know younger women, the very ones you're most concerned with, put you down as a "dirty old man." We've all heard that phrase and it strikes terror into masculine hearts, too.

Well, in most cases, it's appropriate, isn't it? Here you have some old codger who's grizzled and unkempt and smells vaguely of disinfectant and he's eyeing lithesome young things in scanty attire. They see this old letch and turn away in disgust with muttered remarks about dirty old men. And who can blame them?

You are a dirty old man. Go look in a mirror. Would you be favorably impressed by somebody who looks like you? It's a wonder the cops don't arrest you for unnecessary ugliness in a public place.

Go on home and clean up, for God's sake. Put on a clean shirt and a nifty sport coat and throw those shoulders back. Lose that beer belly that o'er hangs your belt like a pending avalanche and adopt the slim look of a guy who's still in shape. It'll make a world of difference in how women perceive you

Ever notice how some old dudes have these good-looking dames on their arms all the time? They're your age and beyond but they still cut a wide swath amongst the widows around town. Why are they more successful than you? Could it be because they don't look like dirty old men and you do?

Incidentally, the same applies to women. You want some male company? Is there some guy at the bridge club you'd like to lure into a romantic entanglement? Want to make an impression on the UPS driver? It's easy, just make the necessary changes and you'll be half way home.

So trade in the Eddie Bauer catalogue for one of the better department stores and dress up a bit more than down. Pretend you still count. Wear an air of prosperity and hold your head high. Keep your hands in your pockets when your Parkinson's kicks up and try to create the impression of vigor with a devil-may-care swagger.

You'll be astonished at the results—and some of the luckier ones might even score now and then.

Survival Rules
1. You're old so you can do anything.
    a. Wear sneakers and jeans seven days a week.
    b. Opt for sensible shoes and muumuus.
    c. Stress comfort and ease.
2. But watch for signs of senility.

a. Gravy stains on your shirt.
   b. Miss-buttoned sweaters.
   c. Mismatched shoes.
3. Contrarily, dress up, not down for increased respect.
4. Avoid the "dirty old man" syndrome. Neatly dressed guys will score more often.
5. Women, too. Get out the high heels and uplift bras.
6. Put on a new mental attitude with your new duds.

CHAPTER FOURTEEN

Plastic Surgery

An adjunct to the preceding chapter has to do with plastic surgery as an alternative for old people. The question is should you have your physiognomy reworked by the surgeon's knife or go through what remains of your life with jowls like a bloodhound and boobs resembling fried eggs?

I say opt for the knife.

Look, we just saw how important one's appearance can be for success in the modern world. People judge you by how you look. Okay, you look like hell and there's a way you can be made beautiful or handsome again so why not go for it?

Age wreaks havoc with our appearance. Wrinkles the size of miniature Grand Canyons show up in once flawless faces. Laugh lines so deep they bring tears to your eyes surround your mouth. Your brow is so furrowed it looks like Farmer Jones has just prepared it for the spring planting.

Noses grow longer with age and tend to hook a bit. Bags, no, portmanteaus, appear under your eyes. Three or four chins now hang where only one hung not too long ago. There are brown liver spots all over your hands, some of them linked with ink lines where one of your grandkids has been playing connect-the-dot. Ears become enormous appendages on either side of your head and begin to look like bookends holding your head up.

In short, you're eighty-something and look every minute of it. But you aren't eighty-something inside. You feel like a mere stripling of fifty or so. What to do?

Years ago there was nothing to do. People just got old and looked it. In fact, most of them looked old when they were in their forties and were stuck with it. Modern science has changed all that.

Remember Phyllis Diller? The comedienne? This woman must be at least ninety-six and yet she looks great today. I saw her on TV not long ago and there's not a line in the woman's face. Her skin is taut as a drum. Her neck is smooth, her brow un-furrowed. I understand she's had her boobs reupholstered, her hips planed down, her nose chiseled into shape, her thighs retooled, her calves mitered, and even her feet sanded and buffed.

The woman hardly has any original parts left. Everything's been replaced or revamped or redesigned. She's packed with various gels and silicone and sundry stuffing to the point where no one knows where Phyllis leaves off and the artificial components begin. And she looks great!

So who cares if the woman is 70% plastic and putty and glue? She looks wonderful, even better than she did twenty or thirty years ago, and she owes it all to her surgeon. Where's the harm?

By all means, consider plastic surgery. Go see your doctor and sign up for the works. Pick out a new nose from the catalogue, one that isn't bent or curved like a scimitar. Do something about those chins. Have that beer belly liposuctioned flat. Chop Lyndon Johnson's ears down to size. And what about those boobs?

Just think what a hit you ladies can be around the bridge club if you show up with a set of thirty-eights standing up like twin sentinels for all to see! Imagine reaching across the table to retrieve an errant card with enough cleavage showing to alarm Ray Charles. Why, you'd be the talk of the place and the envy of everyone there. Other women would regard you as a shameless hussy and draw themselves up indignantly whenever you showed up.

Wouldn't that be great?

And wouldn't you be popular with the men! Why, every old duffer in the neighborhood would gaze on you in silent awe. Like President Carter, they'd lust after you in their hearts and the bolder of them, the ones still able to get it up, would hustle you like a lot of gigolos after an heiress. Overnight you'd be a femme fatale again, and all because you pumped some stuffing into your boobs.

The truth is if you have enough money you can be made over into almost any form that strikes your fancy. There's no need to wear yourself out in some sweaty gym and invite heart attacks through over exertion; no, you just put yourself in the hands of a competent plastic surgeon and presto! You're young and beautiful again.

Are there risks to all this surgery? Sure, but you're eighty-years old. Who cares? What if you elect to have that boob job or your beak reworked and your heart gives out on the operating table? So what? You're already in Grim's sights in any case, aren't you? You can hear his printer clacking away, the soft rustle of computer paper endlessly folding itself into a neat pile as your name moves ever closer to the top of the list.

So what if the silicone drifts around and clogs your plumbing and kills you ten years down the road? Chances are you won't live ten years, anyway. Where's the risk?

What if you have all this work done and it only lasts for five or six years? It's still okay. Five years is long enough if you're eighty. It's much tougher on young people who have to have themselves remodeled every five or six years because everything slips and slides around and needs touching up periodically.

Why look like an old-timer on the brink of death or worse when you can look good again, even young again? Stand naked in front of a full-length mirror and take inventory of your various parts. (Be sure the shades are drawn, as we don't want to alarm passersby.) Size yourself up. Which parts need overhauling? What are your weakest points? Sometimes you can arrange a package deal and get a lower rate for the work done.

So hie yourself down to the doctor and order your new parts. It's all the rage, everybody's doing it. Then lean across that card table and watch their eyes pop, by God.

Survival Rules
    1. Plastic surgery is okay for old folks. Slice away.
    2. Get a boob job. You'll be the hit of your condo.
    3. Bob those Lyndon Johnson ears.

4. Move your fat around so it's more evenly distributed.
5. Choose plastic surgery over exercise every time.
6. Have everything overhauled at once and try to get a bulk rate.

CHAPTER FIFTEEN

Travel

What about travel? Is it a good thing for old folks to go traipsing all over creation in tourist buses and chartered airplanes in an effort to add some spice to their otherwise dreary lives?

Of course it is. I heartily recommend travel for old people if only because it's a good idea to offer Grim a moving target and keep him confused. As it is, Grim has a bead on you and you know he's closing in even as we speak. Once you appear on his screen he'll swoop in and round you up just as he did all those dead friends of yours.

You can throw him off if you step lively enough. Make reservations to tour one of those mountain villages in the Caucasus where hardly anybody ever dies and Grim could lose you for years as he so seldom does any business in those places.

This isn't to say you can evade Grim for sure, though, as he's known to have agents working territories all over the planet and beyond and any of them could round you up in his stead. I knew one guy in his nineties who hopped a jet when he heard Grim was in the neighborhood and fled to a remote Alaskan fishing village only to run smack into one of Grim's agents named Epstein the minute he landed. He was coming down the steps from the plane when he spotted the grinning Epstein and he was so startled he fell and landed on his heart and broke it. The autopsy showed he died of a broken heart but in truth his death was due to an efficient computer and the wonders of modern technology.

Still, you'll have better odds if you aren't a stationary target so pack those bags and give Grim a run for his money.

Evading Grim aside, travel is good for its own sake. Visiting new places takes your mind off other things and gives you a little breathing room. Circumnavigate the globe and forget your troubles in transit. Sign up for a cruise and meet new people. While it's true these new people won't be any different or better than the people you know at home, at least they'll be new.

As none of them will know you, you can pretend you're somebody you're not and bask in an artificial glow of prominence denied you at home. Tell them you're related to some famous person and demand deference. Regale them with stories of imaginary White House visits and assignations with famous movie stars in your youth. You can be whatever you want to be in a strange land and have the time of your life in the bargain.

If you do go, get your money's worth. Dare to be different, do memorable things that will expand your horizons intellectually and emotionally. Run with the bulls at Pamplona a la Hemingway, et al. If you're lucky enough to get a clean horn wound through your thigh, just think what a story that'll make back home at the Rotary meeting.

It'd be an especially interesting story, so interesting

that it would make all the major news services, if you ran with those bulls while using a walker. Can't you see the footage on TV? Fierce bulls rushing through the streets, razor sharp horns hooking this way and that, and you hurtling along in front of them with your walker as the bulls overtake you and…

You must admit it would make mighty dramatic footage, wouldn't it?

Avoid guided tours. For one thing they go too fast and you'll never keep up.

What's more, you have to go where they want to go and you can only stay as long as they let you. Suppose you drop in on the Follies and you're on a tour. Why, with your luck the driver won't give you more than an hour or so to soak up a little genuine French culture before ordering you back on the bus in order to rush you over to somebody's botanical gardens or stupid wax museum.

But if you go on your own you can linger at the Follies for days and see things that are really worth seeing. You'll also miss all those botanical gardens and stupid wax museums and that alone justifies traveling solo.

All in all, then, travel can be a rewarding experience. Lots of people over sixty-five rove the planet in droves and claim to love every minute of it. Most of them even make it back home in more or less one piece and eagerly look forward to future travels. It may work as well for you.

Still, be forewarned. Travel can be a drag. Ten hours in a crowded jet en route to Europe is no vacation.

Lost luggage and Italian pickpockets and 50,000,000 arrogant Frenchmen may prove less entertaining than you'd hoped.

Things can be especially tough for octogenarians. A walking tour of the Left Bank or climbing the pyramids at Giza could easily tax an old-timer's strength unless he happened to be in top shape. Even the dancing girls at the Follies Bergere may prove too much for an old codger who's had two or three open heart surgeries and wears a pacemaker.

And don't forget all that foreign food. Italian pasta and German sauerkraut and French snails combined with Swedish meatballs, Spanish bouillabaisse, and Norwegian codfish balls could do serious harm to your digestive tract for months to come. Add some Japanese sushi and you're guaranteed an attack of something.

Living out of suitcases is hard, too, even for younger people in top form. The stress of being on the move for weeks on end can be tough on people more accustomed to lounging in rockers with movement limited to brief forays to the refrigerator for another beer.

The fact is even though I encourage others to travel hither and yon, I much prefer staying home. I figure if I haven't seen it by now I'm just going to have to give it a miss, that's all. For one thing, I hate flying. Nobody's convinced me yet that flying is actually possible let alone something a sane man will do. You can't tell me those planes aren't falling out of the skies like so many rocks in a series of crashes that are routinely hushed up by the media to protect the interests of the airlines.

We only hear about the obvious crashes like the ones that fall on New York or downtown L.A., the ones they can't hush up because half the world saw them go down. Those planes that run into remote mountains and disappear into the seas are never reported, their flight numbers blipped off computer screens in the terminals and their very existence denied by the authorities.

But flying aside, I stay home because there's no place like it. I have everything I need or want within a thirty-minute drive. While it's true there are no pyramids within thirty minutes of my house, or Taj Mahals, Great Walls, Left Banks, Grand Canals or Andean ruins, it's also true that I don't need or want these things. So why risk life and limb to see things I don't particularly want to see?

Remember, Thoreau never traveled more than fifty miles from Concord in his entire life and he seems to have been a fairly well rounded guy. Hey, if it's good enough for Thoreau, it's good enough for me, by God.

Still, lots of people love traveling and will bear any hardship to go anywhere at all. Their idea of bliss is riding a Mexican bus down the side of a mountain with farmers holding live chickens and goats for traveling companions. Nothing stops them. Not pickpockets or earthquakes or crashing planes or Montezuma's revenge or lost luggage.

They're welcome to it and so are you. If traveling is your thing, then pack up and get on that plane. Who cares if you're old and bordering on senility? You sure as hell won't be any younger or saner if you don't go, you know.

Send me a postcard but don't add the usual wish you were here stuff. I'm glad I'm not there.

Survival Rules
1. Travel is good for old-timers. It makes it harder for Grim to find you.
2. Take a cruise and score one more time.
3. Do daring things such as running with the bulls at Pamplona.
4. Avoid guided tours, as they're full of old people who'll slow you down.
5. On the other hand, consider staying home. It's less fatiguing.
6. If you get the travel bug, reread Thoreau.

CHAPTER SIXTEEN

Condos/Clubs

When most people retire they hurry down to Florida or Arizona, buy a condo, and lie around doing nothing for a month or so because they think this is what retirement is all about. Then they get bored and start looking around for something to do. And then they join clubs because that's where everybody else is.

Let me give you some advice that will stand you in good stead in this phase of your life. First, be sure you choose a club that meets your needs. If you get off on outdoor stuff then align yourself with the shuffleboard crowd or sign up for golf outings. Join the fishermen's league or the lawn bowlers and soak up those rays.

If you're more into intellectual stuff then see if there's a chess club nearby or maybe a discussion group. You'll want to be sure you can play chess and speak intelligently, of course, or you'll be exposed as a half-wit and four-flusher and be shunned by condo dwellers everywhere.

When you actually approach the club for the first time, lie about your background. You see, all social groups establish hierarchies, a kind of pecking order so they'll all know who's who and who defers to whom. If you join up and announce you're a retired cop, say, people will know to treat you as a public servant, a personage of lesser importance than a doctor, for example.

Now we all know this is so much crap, don't

we? What should really count is whom you are and not what you are. Isn't that the very foundation of our democracy? So these phonies want to sort you out by job and bank account and assign you a social position that will be your lot for the rest of your life?

Nonsense. Don't fall for it. Tell them you're an erstwhile banker. Claim you were a vice-president. This is especially believable because all bankers are vice-presidents, even the clerks. Learn a few bank phrases such as mortgage, loan, FCC, interest, amortization, and checking account. Have a blue pinstriped suit with a vest and wear it now and then to reinforce the image.

The club members will be duly impressed and assign you a lofty spot in the hierarchy and you'll be treated favorably ever after. The club bigwigs will invite you to dinner and ask you to sit at their tables at all dinner dances and similar soirees. You'll be a member of the so-called "in" group and all because you had the good sense to lie right from the start.

Tell these arrogant elitists you're a former cop and they'll ask you to guard the parking lot on meeting nights. Your wife will be assigned to the clean-up squad after every luncheon and you'll never get within shouting distance of the "in" group table. All you have to do is plan ahead.

Whatever your background, if it can be improved on, then do so. Avoid all blue-collar work. Never admit you got your hands dirty as these humbugs scorn people who actually do any real work. If you drove a truck, tell them you owned a trucking line. You were a sewer worker? Say you were an engineer specializing in subterranean projects. You ran a mom and pop grocery store? Insist it was a supermarket.

See how it works? Oh, they're lies, all right, but what harm do they do? Is it right or fair for these nitwits to relegate you to an inferior social position because you were an honest worker and not a lord with an inherited title? Such an act is unjust and your innocent lie will right a grievous wrong.

You have to be careful about certain professional careers that are anathema everywhere. You were a dentist? Claim you were a bond salesman, as nobody likes dentists because they associate them with pain and palpable fear. In fact, they may even blackball you if they find out you fixed teeth for a living. A mortician? Same thing. Who wants to hang around guys who muck about with dead people?

So it is with lawyers. Never admit to being an attorney, not if you ever want to hold your head up in that condo again. People will forgive almost anything eventually, but nothing as unpardonable as having once practiced law. A politician? Don't be silly. Why would anyone want to spend time with someone utterly devoid of scruples and integrity? Tell them you sold used cars and you'll be further ahead.

But you see how it goes. With a little carefully contrived maneuvering you may even end up president of the club and then you can blackball new members who aren't quite your social equals. Isn't that the American way?

But what if they ask probing questions designed

to unmask you? Don't answer them. Either that or be evasive. Bob and weave. Dazzle them with footwork. Tell them you swore when you retired that you'd never again have anything to do with banking, flying, deep-sea diving or whatever it was you told them you did. Say you took an oath, a sacred pledge, and you never break a vow.

Willingly discuss anything but your phony career. People will come to accept you at your word and even mark you down as a bit eccentric but you'll be safe with your secret.

By the way, the same advice holds true for widows. They should lie about their deceased husbands' careers for the same reason. It's a lot better to be the widow of a banker than a cab driver. All the same benefits apply.

But what if you're found out finally? Suppose it gets out that you're not a duchess but an erstwhile charwoman? Not a banker but a cab driver? So what? Stand tall and look the old biddies right in the face and tell them to get lost. Refuse to apologize. Insist you were driven from Russia or Samarqand or the wilds of Tibet after a coup and only took a lowly job because your royal upbringing made you too proud to accept charity.

In fact, go on the attack. Tell them you've been slumming anyway and henceforth you'll associate only with select people who are worthy of the attention of a royal personage such as yourself. Being the superficial people they are, they'll all be vying with each other to be included in your retinue and you'll end up with an even more exalted position than before.

Okay, you've established yourself as a person of consequence in the life of the condo and have infiltrated a club or two. That's good but be careful you don't overdo it. Don't join the condo governing board, a mistake many new retirees make and live to regret.

No matter what you do or how hard you work the ungrateful scoundrels will be narking at you throughout your entire term. It's your fault if somebody makes too much noise or parks in the wrong slot or steals people's newspapers or has a cat that pisses in other people's flowerpots and on and on.

They'll drive you nuts. Most of them will be women, of course, since all their husbands have long since been killed off, and they'll plague you with complaints that Judge Learned Hand couldn't handle. In fact, I've known of a number of cases where the members of the condo board were sued by disgruntled tenants and the poor bastards had to hire lawyers and mortgage their units to pay their legal bills.

It's a thankless job so don't you take it.

Another thing, buy the kind of condo where they don't allow anyone under forty or so. And don't worry about the half-wits who insist such restrictions are illegal and periodically file suits to allow them to bring in six or seven spoiled brats and fill the place with chaos and mayhem. These adults-only condos have gone to court and won the right to discriminate on the basis of age because even the judges know what a pain in the ass a lot of noisy kids can be.

Try to get a unit next door to a retired doctor, a

heart specialist, if possible, so he'll be close by when your ticker conks out on you. It's also a good idea to get a unit on one of the upper floors so you can get a telescope and zero in on all the ladies in nearby units. This is convenient if you've joined the Window Peepers club as you can hold meetings at your place and still do meaningful fieldwork without leaving the living room.

All you widowers out there should make a practice of flirting with all the women in the place for two reasons. First, it would be an act of kindness to add a new dimension to the lives of a dozen or more lonely widows who would be thrilled at the attention. These women have often given up any thought of romance and things sexual and the mere thought of such possibilities would stir forgotten emotions and add excitement and even intrigue to their lives.

In fact, if you're still virile and/or have gone the penile implant route or are on Viagra you'd be doing them a service to, uh, well, service them while you're at it. Believe me, you'd be the most popular guy in the place within a fortnight as word spread like wildfire through the widow population. It would be a humanitarian act, a selfless act, a kind act, even.

Yes, ladies can play this game, too. Get your hair done and lay in a supply of black garter belts and lacy stuff. Dig out those spike heels and nylons and wash in some exotic perfume and practice batting those eyes. Show them a well-turned ankle. Lean over a lot and expose as much cleavage as you can muster. Ask the widower next door to come in and help you move some things. Get in the closet with him and make the moves that'll get his attention if he isn't utterly hopeless and you can turn an otherwise empty afternoon into a memorable event.

Remember, guys are easy marks. Show a guy a little thigh and put a hand on the old fool's knee and bam! He's yours to do with as you will. Isn't that a pleasant thought?

A second reason for widowers to romance the ladies is that you'll never have to cook again or even go grocery shopping. Widows all love to feed widowers; it's genetic or something, I guess. In any case, you'll receive endless invitations for breakfast, lunch, and dinner seven days a week. Of course, some of these ladies will be utter failures as cooks but so what? Think of the sunshine and joy you'll bring to their empty lives by deigning to let them feed you.

Incredible.

We could go on indefinitely but you get the picture. Life in a condo in the 21st century can be dreary monotony and crushing boredom if you're the sort of person who values these commodities. On the other hand, the same condo can be a fascinating place offering adventure and excitement and endless variety. Which kind of place you get is entirely up to you.

Survival Rules

1. Choose a club that meets your needs. Don't insist on joining the Phi Beta Kappa alumni bunch if you're an idiot.
2. Lie about your background to achieve higher status.

3. Don't let them know you were something undesirable like a dentist or a mortician.
4. Live in an adults-only community.
5. Flirt with the widows as everyone benefits. You get free home-cooked meals and they get romance back in their lives.
6. Widows should stock up on lacy stuff and garter belts and put some romance back in their own lives.
7. Never serve on a condo board or hold office in a club. You don't need the grief.

CHAPTER SEVENTEEN

Driving (Cheating)

The first thing everybody thinks when you get old is that you're automatically incompetent and helpless and that's disgraceful and not always true. Of course, sometimes it is true, a fact that can be verified just by watching the wacko stuff a lot of old-timers do, but it certainly isn't true in every case. Clearly, you aren't in that category.

Once you hit seventy or so well meaning people are apt to want to put you on the shelf, as it were, and protect you from yourself. This is especially true when it comes to driving.

Turn seventy and have a minor accident and see what happens. Your sappy relatives will demand that you stop driving at once, as you're a danger to yourself and others. They'll usually offer to take your brand-new Lincoln Town Car off your hands as a favor to you, and always at a fraction of what the thing cost.

Resist these blackguards. Tell them you'll let them know when you can't drive anymore, by God. Insist that you're a skillful driver with the reflexes of a teenager. Challenge them to a test drive. Put on a show. Whip that Lincoln into high gear and burn some rubber. Adjust the radio as you drive to display your dexterity and ability to do two or more things at the same time.

Zip into parallel parking spaces with élan. (Since many women can't parallel park, they'll have to forgo this maneuver, of course.) Change lanes without a backward glance to demonstrate your overall confidence in your abilities. Let them know they're dealing with somebody who's still on top of things. If you take a firm stand right from the start, you can convince them you're still a good driver and keep your wheels for many more years to come.

But have a second fender bender after seventy and these same relatives will call the cops on you. Now you've got serious trouble. Cops aren't as easy to fool as your thickheaded relatives and they'll demand more proof that you can drive than your ability to parallel-park a car.

Suppose your eyes have begun to fail, for example. Maybe you've had a bout of cataracts, say, and three-fourths of your eyeball is glazed over like a donut. The truth is you can't see worth a damn. What to do?

Try driving slower. It works. We've all seen some old codger hunched over the steering wheel and squinting like mad as he zips along at 20mph in a 50mph zone. He takes off from lights at a crawl and doesn't even get into second gear before he hits the next light. He's totally unperturbed by irate drivers giving him the finger and honking and passing him on all sides.

This is good for two reasons. For one thing he'll never get a speeding ticket. And, secondly, if he ever does hit anything the damage is likely to be light and therefore inexpensive both in terms of required bodywork and lawsuits by dead pedestrians. You should keep this in mind when you see one of these guys on the road and try not to get too pissed about his driving.

Another thing you can do if your vision isn't very good is to employ a facsimile of the well-known white cane, i.e., drive a white car with the front painted red to warn people that you're blind and to watch the hell out when you show up. Think what a help it would be if everyone who couldn't see drove such a car. Pedestrians could wave them through intersections when the coast was clear and see them coming and get out of their way.

They could have special plates announcing their deficiency and even get decals to allow them to park in handicapped places. After all, we still live in a democracy and these people have a right to drive just as every good American.

It's a question of civil rights, in fact. We routinely allow inmates of asylums to vote in elections, don't we? And don't we print ballots so every illegal alien can vote in whatever language he speaks? Death row inmates claim a right to father children, congressmen assert a God-given right to steal and lie, churches claim the right to tell us how to live. So why don't advanced cataract patients have as much right to drive a car as anyone else?

You can also trick them into thinking you can see like a hawk by cheating on your eye exam. Hang around the DMV office and memorize the eye chart. Get some binoculars and sit in an inconspicuous place and study the thing. Once you've got it down pat, renew that license and rattle off those letters like a tourist from the planet Krypton.

Or wear a headset wired to a confederate standing nearby, someone who can see, of course, and have him whisper the letters into your ear as you study the chart. Or again, have somebody take the test for you. Get somebody who's about your age and sex and let him stand-in for you. The only hard part will be finding a way to get your own picture taken instead of his but you'll have to work that out for yourself.

What if you've had two or three heart surgeries and suffer frequent fainting spells? Is that any reason to strip you of your driving license? I think not. After all, the question is how well you drive when you aren't having a spell, isn't it? Besides, maybe you'll have all your fainting spells when you aren't driving. In that case, wouldn't you suffer needlessly if they took away your license?

Okay, but suppose they get tough and take your driver's license away, anyway. Does that mean you can't drive anymore? Of course not. There are millions of people driving out there on suspended licenses and nothing ever happens to them. We read about it every day in the papers. Some dimwit is arrested on his fourth drunk driving charge and we learn his license was suspended three arrests ago. Does he go to jail?

Are you kidding? He's given a stern warning, a stiff fine, and told never to drive again. The guy pays the fine, swears he'll give up driving, and then goes out and climbs in his car and drives off. Where's the justice?

Another ruse is to enlist other blind and spell-prone old-timers and form up car pools. This is especially good if at least one of you has a valid license since you can always claim he was driving whenever you hit something. After the accident you all pile out at once and point ol' Ed out as the driver. Witnesses won't trip you up as all old people look alike and they won't be able to tell one from another.

Act confused when the cops show up and they'll assume you're senile and take your word for it. Ol' Ed probably won't even know whether he was driving or not so how could the cops hope to sort it out?

Still another dodge that could work if they take away your driver's license is to get a motorcycle license and drive a Harley. I believe the rules for motorcycle drivers are different than for a regular license. For one thing you aren't required to be as smart since everyone knows Harley riders are usually illiterate and often bereft of common sense. You're also allowed to have less acute vision as bikers usually have a lot of dead bugs in their eyes, anyway, so what difference does it make if they can't see all that well?

Or ride one of those little scooters the kids use. These things don't require any license, as they're nothing more than bicycles with a motor attached. You can even ride the damn things on the sidewalk. They're also easy to park and will fit into the smallest spot in the lot right up next to the entrance. It's like having a handicap permit only better since even handicappers require a full-size parking slot.

The point is it's a real pain if you can't drive

nowadays. To take away a man's driver's license is to deny him full citizenship and deprive him of any chance to lead a normal life.

You'll have trouble getting dates because nobody wants to go out with a guy who can't drive a car. People will have to chauffeur you around and they'll resent it. If your wife's doing all the driving, she'll know every place you go and it'll be nearly impossible to carry on an affair with the widow across town.

You could even have to end up taking the bus and the very idea of that is unthinkable. Could anything be more demoralizing?

So fight them. Hang on to that license with might and main. Insist you're a good driver still and keep driving as long as you can back the car out of the garage and swing her out into traffic.

Remember, driving is a right and not a privilege in this country.

Survival Rules
1. Don't let them know you can't see. Fake it.
2. Try to have fainting spells only when you aren't driving.
3. Drive real slow.
4. Try a Harley or a motor scooter.
5. Cheat on the eye test.
6. If they do take your license away, drive anyway. Everybody else does.

CHAPTER EIGHTEEN

Sleeping

If there's one thing most old-timers shouldn't be worried about it's a lack of sleep. The average creaky octogenarian will soon have all the sleep he wants and then some. He's facing Sleep, Unlimited. He might more properly be concerned with an antidote to sleep, some sort of magical No-Nod pill that would neutralize Grim's knockout drops and keep that very long night at bay.

Be that as it may, getting enough sleep is a problem for lots of old people. Some of them fall asleep at will and sleep like a lot of dead guys right through the night and regularly enjoy a solid eight hours of restful sleep. Others can't sleep worth a damn. It's usually one or the other. If you're one of the latter don't skip this chapter as it provides new insights into the problem and you'll miss them if you don't read on.

Most people, even young ones, seem to fall into one of these categories. The lucky ones sleep like Rip Van Winkle and the rest sleep not at all. The patterns are set early in life, apparently, and continue into old age. In other words, most people who are insomniacs at thirty will probably be insomniacs at eighty.

So what do you do if you can't sleep? You do have options. Lots of people stay up late on purpose and defy sleeplessness. Watch the late-night talk shows. See what's playing on the cable movie channels. Listen to one of these all-night radio talk show stations along with the other night owls out there.

You can even call in yourself. Find out which stocks to buy or how to build an addition on your house or how to sue successfully in small-claims court. These shows can be highly informative as well as entertaining and they'll help while away those lonely hours between midnight and first light.

Or you can go out on the town. Get dressed and head for one of the livelier nightspots in your city. Drop by one of the singles' bars and provide a little merriment for the habitués. They'll be astonished to see an old-timer like you in a place where there's never anybody over thirty and you'll be an instant hit.

You'll know you've found the right place if they card you on the way in and try to keep you out on the grounds that you're too old. Don't let them. Demand to see the manager. Tell them you have a bad ticker and it often stops outright if you're frustrated in any way. They'll be afraid you'll drop dead on them and your heirs will sue them into bankruptcy.

Remember our chapter on freedom. Old people have the world by the balls; no one wants to thwart senior citizens, as there's no percentage in it. It's a no-win situation. If you make trouble for old-timers you'll have the AARP on you and a lot of old fogies will be picketing your place while TV cameras record the scene for the evening news.

Insist on dancing. Get up and leap about insofar as such a thing is possible. People will be charmed at your spirit and spunk and they'll buy you drinks and free cigars and slim young things will fight to see who gets the next dance. Pinch their pretty behinds and dance real slowly. Proposition all the good-looking ones and hope none of them take you up on it.

This goes for women, too. Demand that the guys buy you drinks. Threaten to make a scene if they refuse. Grab their thighs under the table and remember to lean over and reveal a lot of cleavage. Pick out a handsome guy and insist that he take you home or else. On the way out ask him if he has any protection and if he doesn't offer him his choice of condoms from your purse.

After listening to loud rock music and dancing with nubile young girls (or virile young men) for an hour or two you'll be so fatigued you'll sleep like a baby. Your only problem will be staying awake long enough to get home.

Yes, I know. Going out late at night can be risky. You could get mugged or even killed. So what? You're past eighty, remember? What have you got to lose?

There are things you can do at home to induce sleep if you really can't make the club scene. There are the old standbys like drinking warm milk or practicing self-hypnosis. The warm milk dodge is no good because milk is bad for people over six and, besides, most people can't stand drinking the stuff.

As for hypnosis, most oldsters are too cynical to be fooled by some sort of mental gymnastics designed to trick the mind into believing something that's patently not true. The old-timers I've known couldn't be conned into falling asleep by Mesmer himself. Still, it's worth a try, especially if you're the gullible sort and easily manipulated. People who believe politicians are excellent candidates for hypnosis for that reason.

Then there are the various chemicals such as are found in sleeping pills. These are barbiturates, generally, and they do work. Pop a couple during the eleven o'clock news and you'll be hard pressed to see the end of the program. You'll sleep like a log the night through and dream remarkable dreams.

The trouble is you'll still be drugged when you wake up. These chemicals lodge themselves in what's left of your brain and linger there for days on end. You'll feel like you spent the night in the Twilight Zone with Rod Serling.

What's more, you build a tolerance for these drugs and need more of them to do the job. Eventually, you end up downing eight or ten a day and still can't get to sleep. All in all, it's probably a better idea to avoid the stuff and get used to tossing and turning four or five hours a night.

One of the best tonics for producing high quality levels of refreshing sleep is to engage in wild, uninhibited, incredibly erotic sex at bedtime. It's even more effective if men manage to enlist the services of beautiful, lithe young women with wondrous bodies who are passionate beyond belief. Women should employ a male stripper, a lean, muscular guy in his twenties who can keep it up interminably.

Rig a mirror over your bed. Put on some Sinatra tapes and light some candles. You could even set up your camcorder and record the event for future reference or to show the ladies at your next bridge party. Then cut loose. Shed your inhibitions with your clothes. Put your heart and soul—and assorted other parts—into it with enthusiasm and wild abandon until you finally explode in a shower of brightly colored rocketry and every last ounce of strength drains from your body in a mind-numbing rush.

Done right, you'll sleep the sleep of the dead and wake in the morning feeling refreshed and revitalized and more alive than a new kitten working on the first of his nine lives.

However, there's another caveat here. Just as sleeping pills can be addictive, so can sex of the kind described above. Lots of old guys have dallied with young women of this sort and been changed into physical and emotional derelicts for their trouble.

I knew one old duffer who used this trick for getting to sleep but he got hooked and couldn't go to sleep at all without a rousing encounter with a nubile young woman. Even more, he convinced himself that if one sexpot was good two would be even better and in no time he was in so deep he needed a well-organized orgy before he could even take a quick mid-afternoon nap.

As the old coot was in his eighties, you can imagine what finally happened. That's right, it killed him in the end. He overdosed is what he did. One night he'd worked his way through three or four young things and was well on his way to the Land of Nod when he decided to have one more for the road, as it were. He did and Grim caught up to him just as he reached the part where the sky filled with exploding rocketry.

Still, he grinned like Alice's Cheshire cat when the paramedics arrived and they recognized his condition at once and refused to revive him. It seems he'd died the perfect death and it was against the paramedics' code to intervene in what was obviously a divinely arranged matter. After all, what would be the point?

So what can we learn from all this? Nothing and everything. It's okay to suffer from insomnia when you're old; in fact, it's even desirable in light of what's waiting for you just around the corner. You should stay awake as long as you can. Train yourself to get along on two or three hours sleep a night. Practice sleeping with one eye open so Grim can't sneak up on you. Drink caffeine-rich coffee just before bedtime and keep the room brightly lighted.

Remember, sleeping can be dangerous to your health, especially deep sleep. How many stories have you heard where some old codger was reported to have died in his sleep? Doesn't that sound a warning bell? Would he have died at all if he hadn't been asleep? Who knows?

The real secret is to avoid sleep. Most people sleep away a full third of their lives as it is and that's the equivalent of being dead for eight hours every day. The less you sleep the longer you live. Encourage insomnia and live longer.

So there you have it. Stay awake and enjoy life. Glory in the light; it's fading quickly enough.

Survival Rules
1. To induce sleep, eschew pills and potions and try unbridled sex. If you still don't get to sleep, you won't care.
2. However, beware of overdosing on sexy young things.
3. Tire yourself out physically by partying with much younger people.
4. Ideally, avoid sleep as it's uncomfortably death-like and Grim may mistake you for a client ready for collection.
5. Stock up on No-Nod pills and caffeine.
6. Remember, life is light and darkness isn't.

CHAPTER NINETEEN

Divorce

Should old people get divorced? Sure, why not? Should you go on living with somebody who's a pain in the neck just because you've been married for fifty or sixty years?

Look, if we've learned one thing so far it's that life isn't over until you make that final rendezvous with Grim and his printouts. As long as Grim hasn't stopped round you're still alive and you have a right, even a duty, to go on living with all the gusto you can dredge up.

You're married to a partner you can't stand? So dump him/her without ceremony. It's easy. Mickey Rooney did it eight times—and he's a Christian. Ring up a good divorce lawyer and draw up the papers. Hire a truck and haul away all the good furniture before the papers are served to get a head start on things. Give up custody of the kids to show your willingness to be fair.

Life is too short to sustain a marriage that's gone sour. We all know that's true for younger people, so why shouldn't it be the same for the retired set? If you're eighty you could easily live twenty more years and so could your mate. Isn't that a horrible thought?

Still, it's true that divorce is a disruptive procedure and causes much grief all around. Are there other options? Of course there are. For one thing, consider palming the old codger off on somebody else.

Suppose you're a woman married to a real loser who drives you nuts and you want to get rid of him. So take him to all sorts of affairs where there are lots of widows and turn him loose. Duck out the back way and give the ladies a chance to make their moves. If these widows run true to form, they'll circle his carcass like vultures drawing a bead on a tourist who's run out of gas in Death Valley and move in for the kill.

The fact that he's already somebody else's husband will only add spice to the whole thing, as everybody knows widows won't hesitate to steal a sister's man if they get half a chance at him. It's all a part of the so-called feminine mystique, a part of being a woman and a widow. With any luck the old fool will fall for one or more of these ladies and leave you in the lurch and you'll be free to enjoy what's left of your life without him.

Or take a job that requires traveling to distant states and you can be on the road for three weeks out of every four. Long-distance trucking might be just the thing.

Or tell him you've got to go stay with your sister in Florida while she recovers from some bogus operation and don't come back. You don't even need a real sister in Florida to make this work. Claim she's a long-lost sister who was abandoned at birth and you've only recently learned of her existence. Oprah has these people on her show every week and that will give your story an air of plausibility.

One of the best dodges of all, though, is to have the old fool committed. It's easy, too. All you have to do is show he's nuts and the boys in the white coats will truck him off to the local booby hatch. Get some of your women friends to swear he's balmy. Invent incidents where he demonstrated senility and have your friends swear they're true.

Claim he talks to inanimate objects. See that his clothes are always stained with food droppings. Encourage a disheveled appearance to make him look even more disorganized and out of control. Once you've laid the groundwork and charged him as a mental incompetent it becomes his job to prove the charges are false and that's hard to do.

If you know a judge, or a crooked lawyer who knows a judge he can bribe, you can have the whole thing done in the twinkling of an eye. You pay off the judge; he signs commitment papers, and presto! The old coot is on his way to the funny farm.

Another advantage to this scheme is that you automatically get all his worldly goods for yourself whereas you'll have to split them if you get a divorce. That makes it worth the effort, doesn't it?

You can also plant illegal drugs on him and call the cops. Tell them he's hooked on the dread marijuana plant and has smoked his brain into fried eggs as in the commercial. He could get life without parole and you'd be rid of him for good and all. Even better, you'd get everything again as felons sent to the big house are stripped of all they own and it goes to their wives.

What about having him done in? There's nothing as final as death, you know, and it leaves no messy arguments as to who owns what. Lots of people, mostly women, are having their mates done in by hired killers. When Oprah isn't showcasing reunions of long lost sisters she's featuring women who've had their husbands knocked off by hit men.

It's simple. You just run an ad in one of those soldier-of-fortune mags and an army of would-be hit men will swamp you with queries. The going rate seems to be ten grand payable half when the contract's let and half when the job's done. Don't give them the whole amount up front or the guy will take off and you'll have to kill the old fogy yourself.

Be careful, though. Half the time the hit man turns out to be an undercover cop who's wired. He'll record the whole transaction and arrest you for soliciting murder and you'll end up in the slammer yourself and your husband will run off with your best friend.

If you can't afford ten grand for a hit man, you'll just have to do the job yourself. It's still easy, though. Just claim the guy was abusive and beat you at regular intervals. Get some of your old biddy friends to lie for you, fake a few bruises, and waylay him when he's asleep. It's a good idea to get him drunk or drugged first so he won't wake up and raise hell when you douse him with gasoline preparatory to incinerating him.

Once he's nicely burned to a crisp, call the cops and claim self-defense. Say you feared for your life, that he swore he was going to kill you just as soon as he was sober enough to stand up, and you had no choice. Juries everywhere routinely buy such bizarre stories nowadays and you'll be acquitted before lunch.

But if you're the squeamish type and unwilling to incinerate the old fool, you may have to go the divorce route, after all. In that event, hire a good lawyer, one without a conscience—which is to say any lawyer—and proceed forthwith. Drum up a lot of phony charges. Line up witnesses who'll lie for you under oath. Try to get compromising pictures of him in flagrante delecto, if possible.

While it's true that divorces are easily obtained these days and any court will gladly grant you a divorce for any reason at all, you'll get a better shake if you can prove he's a cad in the bargain. Remember, the point is to make off with as much of the community property as you can safely steal.

Once you're rid of the old guy you'll be free to move in on some other woman's husband and start all over again with a different model even if he's not really much of an improvement on the one you just got rid of.

What the hell, life is short, after all.

Survival Rules
1. To rid yourself of an unwanted husband
    a. Have him committed as an incompetent.
    b. Frame him with planted contraband.
    c. Foist him off on a passing widow.
    d. Hire a hit man.
    e. Do him in yourself for the price of some gasoline and a bottle of cheap booze to knock him out.
2. If all else fails, divorce him. Make up phony

charges, line up perjurers, steal everything transportable.

3. Once free, go steal somebody else's mate and start over.

CHAPTER TWENTY

Religion

Most of us take religion pretty much for granted when we're thirty or forty because nobody dies at such an age, at least not anybody we know, but we begin to take a closer look at it when we sail past sixty-five and start heading for advanced old age when everybody finally dies.

The thing that does it is that prodigal son bit. Here you have one guy, we'll call him Bill, who toes the line for fifty or sixty years and really lives a first-class, righteous life totally devoid of such sinful things as booze, cigars, sex-crazed blondes, wild parties, erotic thoughts, pool halls, topless bars, and similar temptations that plague Everyman.

He finally dies and goes to his reward. He gets a good seat in heaven, a room with a view, an assigned parking slot near all the action, and membership in the Key Club.

Along comes his brother, Fred, and Fred is the exact opposite of steady ol' Bill. Fred smokes a dozen five-dollar cigars a day, drinks imported single malt Scotch, owns a chain of topless bars, favors sex-crazed blondes over all other women, never has a pure thought, and never goes inside a church.

So Fred falls ill at last and Grim is fast approaching with his infernal printouts and loudly calling Fred's name. Fred quickly summons a priest and tearfully begs forgiveness and promises to live a Christian life from then on—or the next ten minutes he has left. The priest mumbles some Latin, douses Fred's body with a flagon of holy water, and Fred dies.

The next day Bill finds out that Fred has not only been given a room right next door to his own, but he also parks in the next slot and sits next to Bill and even has a membership in the Key Club! Naturally, Bill is pissed and he complains to St. Peter.

"Say, Pete," he says, "what's goin' on here, anyway? I led a good Christian life and my loser brother broke every commandment in the book for sixty years. How come he gets all the same stuff I get?"

Pete shrugs. "That's how it works, Bill," he says. "It's all that last shall be first and the first last stuff. You know, the prodigal son thing. You sign up at the last minute and it's as good as a lifetime of religious fanaticism."

If this is how they're going to run things, can you blame people for putting salvation off until they're old-timers and no longer have any interest in sin? Oh, sure, it's a gamble, all right. A guy may fill a book with the darkest sins imaginable and figure to repent on his eightieth birthday and then die at sixty-two and find himself stoking a furnace for Satan but it's a chance most of us are willing to take.

Stop by any old folks' home and see. Holy men are constantly hurrying in trailing bottles of holy water and beads and sticks of incense as they respond to still another emergency call for last-minute salvation. In fact, from what I've been able to tell, it appears just about everybody is ignoring virtuous living in favor of sin and counting on the prodigal son scenario to save them in the end.

And why not? The actuarial tables show the odds are in their favor. The average life expectancy now is about seventy-seven so most of us are pretty safe until then. So live it up while you can and get religion as you draw near that seventy-seventh birthday.

But that's not your only problem. Of all the world's many religions, which one is the right one? Suppose you're a devout Hare Krishna and follow their dogma to the letter. You drop out of college in your freshman year, break your parents' hearts, and sign up with the franchise in your city. You wear those saffron robes and shave your head and learn to play gongs and tin whistles. You pester people on the streets and scare small children and collect money to buy the head guy still another Rolls Royce.

Then you die, go to heaven, and find out God's a Moslem. Now what? He's prepared a long list of questions based on the Koran, which you have to answer to obtain admittance and you've never read a word of it.

Or suppose you're a Moslem and you memorize the Koran and hide your women and refrain from booze and make regular tours to Mecca and then die and find God's an Episcopalian and he doesn't care a fig about Moslems.

See what you're up against here? There are something like two thousand different religions and sects and all of them claim to have the inside track to the afterlife. They can't all be right, you know. It's safe to say that the vast majority of them are totally wrong and have no more influence with God than you have with your cat.

Remember, this is important. We're dealing with eternity here. A false move and you could devote a lifetime to a bogus religion and end up in hell with everybody else that made the wrong choice. This isn't something we can lightly shrug off. We have to be sure.

One tactic would be to make an in-depth study of every religion out there and see what makes them tick. Are their miracles plausible? Do they offer a prodigal son program? Are they listed in the Encyclopedia of World Religions? How strict are their conversion rules? This can be important as some require circumcision and no sane man is going to allow anything as bizarre as that just to join a new church!

You could visit their holy places. Jerusalem is a good place to begin as three religions claim to have started there and you can kill three birds with one stone, as it were. However, it might be wise to wait until the religiosos frequenting that holiest of holy cities have done with killing and maiming each other before venturing forth.

Spend a weekend in Mecca or drop by Lourdes or visit any airport to gain insight into the Hare Krishnas. Take a room in a Tibetan monastery for a year or two. Chant with Buddhist monks in Thailand or burn joss sticks in Chinese temples or sacrifice young virgins in mountain aeries in Peru or get stoned on high-grade marijuana with Rastafarians and examine the ins and outs of their beliefs.

If you made such a study your life's work you'd have a good chance of sorting them out and coming up with a winner eventually, but how many of us are willing to spend our lives researching the world's religions? Nothing would ever get done; there'd be no time for anything else.

There is a time-saving alternative to the above, a new approach to the problem that would clear everything up at once and free us to get on with our sinning in peace. What's more, it has every bit as good a chance to be right as any of the two thousand-odd religions extant now.

It's this. You may in fact safely assume they're all wrong, every single one of them. Since none of them can provide any sort of rational proof to support its claims, isn't it possible they're all wrong? In fact, isn't it even likely?

Does that mean there is no right religion? Of course not. It only means nobody can ever tell with certainty, every man's guess is as good as the next guy's. And that means your own personal views could be the very ones that actually prevail.

Suppose your views are wrong, though. You die and go to heaven and find out God's a Rosicrucian and He hates everybody except fellow Rosies. So what? Are you any worse off than you would be if you'd practiced voodooism or Shintoism or even Catholicism?

Now think even further. If you assume all two thousand-odd religions are wrong, then there are no rules about hiding your women or abstaining from sex-crazed blondes or practicing celibacy that have any meaning for you. In other words, you can do exactly as you please and enjoy life to its fullest without a care about any final accounting.

Isn't that astonishing?

What's that? That's still too risky for you? Maybe you're right. After all, we don't want to do something stupid and find ourselves denied membership in the Key Club, do we?

It is possible that one of these religions is right and if that's true we'd be in serious trouble. It seems clear that we've got to take out some insurance in case we make a mistake in choosing a religion, and the only way I can think of is to join as many different religions as we can work into our schedule and try to cover our asses by numbers alone.

Get yourself baptized in five or six different churches to increase your chances of including the right one. Keep a jug of holy water on hand at all times. Line your family room with Islamic prayer rugs. Keep a supply of young virgins nearby. Install a prayer wheel and hook it up to a motor so you won't get carpal-tunnel syndrome from spinning the damn thing yourself. Eat magic mushrooms and commune with the spirits, or your cat, whichever is handy.

Keep crosses, crucifixes, and Stars of David all over the place. Hang lucky amulets around your neck and burn incense by the pound. Stock Korans, Bibles, the Upanishads, Kama Sutras, and Books of the Dead in your library. Have lunch with monks, viziers, priests, bishops, visionaries, seers, prophets, and prebendaries generally to cover all the bases.

In other words, cover yourself. If you belong to a dozen or more religions you increase the odds that one of them is the right one and you'll have all the correct answers when you finally do get to heaven.

Still, just to make really sure, when you reach eighty or so and you hear Grim coming up the walk, get on the phone and call the nearest priest. Tell him to explain that prodigal son bit again and sign up as a convert before it's too late.

It's just a little insurance, that's all.

Survival Rules
1. To improve your chances of finding the right religion, choose a dozen or more and follow all of them.
2. Study all religions carefully to avoid a wrong choice.
3. To simplify things invent a religion of your own and make up easy rules.
4. Invest in a prayer wheel and shower heaven with prayers. Who knows? It may work.
5. Fill your house with icons from as many religions as possible as a form of spiritual insurance.
6. Remember the prodigal son deal; it may be your only hope.

CHAPTER TWENTY-ONE

Canes, Walkers, Etc.

As we get older we tend to lose things we once took for granted. There was a time when our skin had elasticity and would bounce back to its original shape when pulled or stretched and now it hangs in loose folds and is about as elastic as putty.

We could once see the minutest detail and now can't see any detail at all. Our hearing is going or already gone. Reflexes? Are you kidding? We can't run as fast or jump as high as we once ran and jumped, not even if we're wearing those Michael Jordan sneakers everyone raves about.

It's all a part of aging, the gradual loss of our senses and physical capabilities over time. These losses become especially noticeable when we lose our locomotive powers and have to rely on various aids to get around.

Take the matter of canes. Sooner or later we all end up on a cane if we live long enough. Break a hip in a fall or wrench a knee or twist an ankle and you'll find yourself shopping for a cane. Are there any rules about canes that you may find useful, some sort of cane etiquette you should know? Is one cane better than another?

For openers, it's considered inappropriate to use a white cane with a red tip unless you're actually blind. The blind resent people who aren't blind using their special canes, or they would if they could see such infractions. Of course, if you're using a red-tipped white cane in your work as a street beggar or feigning blindness to induce people to buy your wares through sympathy, then that's different. All others should eschew these special canes.

You'll want to be careful with your cane, too. Don't leave it sticking out in aisles where others can trip over it. Don't wave it around in a careless manner lest you rap some poor sap in the gob with it and get the thing wrapped around your neck for your trouble. And don't threaten people with it unless they really deserve it.

There are all sorts of canes, of course, and you'll want to choose one that's right for you. Suppose you live in a so-called bad part of town, the part where all the muggers and stick-up men live. In that case you might be wise to choose one of the nifty sword canes they sell nowadays.

You buy a conventional looking cane designed for walking. It has a rubber tip on the end and is long enough to reach the ground. The only difference between this cane and regular canes is that this one hides a two-foot long sword in its barrel. A quick twist of the handle and presto! You have a razor sharp sword capable of eviscerating Hulk Hogan himself.

Suppose you're walking down the street late at night and a thug steps from the shadows brandishing a stick and demands your money.

"Gimme your dough, you old fart!" he declares.

"Up yours!" you counter, and quick as a flash you whip out your sword and run the bastard through.

Imagine his surprise! He thinks he's robbing a helpless old fogy and he ends up skewered and bleeding like the proverbial stuck pig as you scamper away with your money intact and an evil laugh echoing behind you as you go.

Isn't that a pleasant scene, though?

If you're reluctant to skewer thugs or lack the strength to thrust with enough force to drive the blade through his worthless hide, you can also buy gun canes. They work the same as a sword cane except there's a working gun inside. The same quick twist and you can drill the bastard through with a high-caliber bullet and attain the same astonished look on his ugly mug as we saw on the stuckee.

An Irish shillelagh is a good choice if you're more interested in bludgeoning people than you are in running them through or shooting them dead. These sticks are made from the tough blackthorn tree and are as sturdy as an iron rod. Shillelaghs make good walking sticks and provide a certain panache that will add a nice twist to your character.

Canes with a crook in them are handy for hanging over your arm while you do something else that requires both hands. You can also trip people with them as Charlie Chaplin was forever doing with his famous Malacca cane.

Any good cane can add a sense of style as you move along the street. Swing it as you go. Put it on your shoulder like a gun and simulate marching in place when Old Glory passes by. Turn it upside down and take practice golf swings a la Johnny Carson ending his monologue. Let a cane become a kind of logo, an adjunct of your personality that will set you apart from people without canes. Use your cane as George Burns used cigars or Tom Wolfe uses white suits.

Use it for other things besides walking. You can push elevator buttons with your cane, flag down cabs, and point out things of interest. Lean heavily on it and reflect phony jolts of pain in your face to enlist compassion from strangers and maybe get a seat on the bus. Use it to fend off vicious dogs while taking afternoon walks and wallop their owners if they complain because you whacked their mutts for them.

A snappy cane can be a colorful addition to your overall image and add an element of style. You might consider getting one even if you don't actually need it yet. Who among us can't use a little additional style and color?

What about walkers? Can you do anything to spice up the average walker? Sure. Buy a designer model, one with racing stripes. Get one with chrome wheels. Paint the thing in gaudy colors and stick little American flags on its corners. Build-in some pockets so you can carry stuff in them and leave your hands free to operate the walker.

Install a leather-covered handle on it. Special order one with some sort of rare Malaysian wood to make it stand out from the other walkers when they're lined up outside the doctor's office. Have your Social Security number carved in it so the police can identify it if stolen.

Above all, learn to operate the thing with style

and verve. Practice taking corners on two wheels and steering with one hand while waving nonchalantly with the other. Take lots of time crossing streets in heavy traffic to avoid falling down and being run over. Ignore the blaring horns and shaking fists of impatient drivers as they're hopeless jackasses who resent you for growing old and inconveniencing them.

Remember, everybody is a mere step away from having a walker of his very own—they just don't know it, that's all.

And wheelchairs? Until recently, these things were a disaster. Not long ago the average wheelchair weighed upwards of a hundred pounds and had all the maneuverability of a grocery cart with badly canted wheels. You had to be Arnold Schwarzenegger to make one of the damn things go. They were uncomfortable and clunky and ugly.

That's all changed now. Wheelchairs today are made from super strong light alloys and scientifically designed for speed and looks. They're light and highly maneuverable and comfortable. Lots of people use them in marathons and even to play tennis and basketball.

Get one with a motor, a big motor, say about 50 hp. You'll be able to zip along sidewalks and through shopping malls like Barney Oldfield in Ol' 99. Some of them even have all-terrain tires so you can ride through swamps with impunity. See if you can add a gearshift for greater power and ask about a turbo system.

And don't be afraid to drive the thing with élan. Race around at high speeds and lean into the turns. Put a horn on it, one of those they use on the big rigs, and toot like mad as you career through the mall. Defy the cops. After all, what judge would uphold a charge of wheelchair speeding against an octogenarian?

Another thing. Agitate for ramps and elevators and special buses equipped to handle wheelchairs. Write your congressman and threaten to get the AARP on him if he doesn't get with it. Petition storeowners to install ramps. If they refuse threaten to fall and break a hip in their store and sue them into bankruptcy.

Nobody wants to require walkers and wheelchairs but a lot of us ultimately do. Some day it'll be your turn. Write that letter now.

Survival Rules

1. Canes add style and panache. Carry one even if you don't need it.
2. Avoid red-tipped white ones unless actually blind.
3. Consider sword canes for stabbing some people and shillelaghs for bashing others.
4. Streamline your walker and operate it with verve.
5. Order a custom-made wheelchair with all the latest innovations on it to impress others.
6. Buy a mechanized chair with lots of power. Drive fast, even recklessly. At your age you've nothing to lose.
7. Demand better facilities for handicapped people as a matter of principle. It could easily be a self-serving move in the long run.

CHAPTER TWENTY-TWO

Shoplifting Seniors

What gives? A chapter on shoplifting? Are we advocating senior citizen theft? Damn right we are!

Look, this has to do with all the really poor seniors out there, the ones retired on minuscule pensions and tiny stock portfolios and skimpy Social Security checks. These people number in the millions and can be found in every large city and hamlet in the country, and they're living substandard lives in one of the richest countries on the planet.

There's been a lot of talk here lately about how our old-timers are such an affluent bunch, people with lucrative investments and generous pensions pouring money into the retirees' coffers every month like clockwork. We hear about their buying power and political influence and condo lifestyles and senior citizen cruises and safe-deposit boxes and people get the impression the nation's elderly are living the life of Riley.

Are there some rich retirees? Certainly. This country is full of retired Teamster officers, Mafia dons, TV evangelists, double-dipping congressmen, crooked mayors, unscrupulous legislators, fraudulent stockbrokers, tinhorn hucksters, sweatshop owners, and kindred souls from a thousand other rackets.

But their numbers are greatly exceeded by all the penurious school teachers, secretaries, hotel doormen, cab drivers, cops, factory stiffs, longshoremen, housewives, and myriad others who eke out a precarious existence on income that would shame a Third World refugee.

Many of our elderly live in homes that would be declared unfit for human habitation in Haiti. Stories of old people eating dog food are not entirely exaggerated. They lack basic nutrition and it shows in their overall health and they don't get proper medical care because they don't have insurance and can't afford the high cost of medicine without it.

Isn't all this disgraceful? Shouldn't we be ashamed? For God's sake, even backward countries populated by infidels manage to provide national health care for their citizens. Shouldn't a nation of Christians do as much?

What can we do about it? Is there a course of action open to old-timers who are down on their luck, hungry and sick and broke? You're damn right there is!

It's simple, really. Remember our earlier chapter on freedom? We agreed that people who've slipped into their dotage and are steadily rising on Grim's printouts are people with nothing to lose because they're staring death in the face and can't be hurt any worse than they hurt now. This is their strength, their ace in the hole, their trump card. Like Gandhi, they're actually strong because they're so weak.

As we saw earlier, the secret is to take what's legitimately yours. If we're agreed that every person in America is entitled to a basic living standard, one that includes adequate food and health care and decent housing—and who would gainsay this?—then it follows that people should simply demand these things and take them by force if necessary.

So here's the plan. Shoplift. Steal food. Visit your local supermarket and purloin some beans and rice and bread. Wear an enormous coat with pockets everywhere and stuff them full of comestibles. What the hell, you won't even need a shopping cart. Go down the aisles with a list so you won't forget anything. Remember, you're only taking what's rightfully yours, anyway.

Have a care, though. Don't steal caviar and malt whiskies and the better cuts of meat. The nation owes you a decent living standard but it doesn't owe you a cornucopia of luxury items. It's one thing to steal food because you're hungry and it's quite another to steal delicacies for your granddaughter's coming out party.

Confine your theft to essential foodstuffs with, maybe, an occasional six-pack thrown in for variety since it's well known that men don't live by bread alone. And steal just enough to feed you and your mate. No fair backing a truck up to the produce department and hauling away a truck full of vegetables. You aren't to sell your booty for profit on the open market, as this would make you a crook in the classic sense and bode ill for a defense based on equity.

For you will be caught. Someone will eventually notice your bulging pockets as you pass through the checkout counter with a loaf of bread and some milk in hand and eighty bucks worth of groceries hidden about your person.

"Oh, how mortifying!" some will say. "Imagine being busted for shoplifting in your local supermarket. Everybody would gather around and point you out to their kids, the store personnel would frown and call the cops and you'd be handcuffed and led away in disgrace!"

Wrong. Nothing of the sort will happen. Hold your head up high and look them straight in the eye and maintain your dignity. Stealing to eat is no crime anywhere on Earth. If anything, your neighbors should be ashamed to live in a society where such a thing could happen.

And therein lies your defense. Remember your age. Nobody can do anything to an octogenarian, especially a hungry one. When you're caught with the goods don't hide and hang your head; instead, call out loudly that you're old and hungry and you only steal to eat. Demand that the press be called, as you want your picture in handcuffs in the papers along with the details of society's crime. Raise Cain. Try to make the cops club you as they're hauling you away. Foam at the mouth and sob uncontrollably and milk the scene for all it's worth. Have an accomplice stand by with his video cell phone and film the entire event for the eleven o'clock news and the upcoming trial.

Refuse bail and demand to be imprisoned while awaiting trial. They're required to feed you in jail and at least you'll get something to eat.

Insist on a jury trial. Demand a free attorney and move that TV cameras be allowed in the court. Sign up a good PR firm to exploit the situation and get you on the talk shows so you can tell your story to the entire nation. See if you can extort some cash from the tabloids or sell your story to some hokey news show.

Your defense will be that even though you've admittedly lived longer than was good for you—or the country—you still have a right to eat and if you can obtain food only by stealing then stealing is no crime and you should be freed withal.

You may rest assured that you'll be freed. No judge would hold you over, no prosecutor would prosecute you or jury would convict you. Your friends and neighbors would be outraged, the press would have a field day, and you'd be a national hero overnight.

See how it works?

Use the same tactics for medical care. If you need an operation and don't have any insurance, break into a nearby hospital and demand to see a surgeon. Chain yourself to a post and hold aloft a phial of nitroglycerin and threaten to level the place if they don't rustle up that surgeon pretty quick.

Don't use real nitro, of course. If you use the real thing they'll classify you as a nut case and they'd be right. It's okay to use plain water, as everybody will gladly take your word for it when you claim its nitro.

Think how that would look on the evening news. The networks would feature you and your nitro in six and eleven o'clock editions. Congressmen would sense an opportunity to advance their careers and the scoundrels would emerge from the woodwork like cockroaches fleeing the fumes of the fumigator. The governor would call. Doctors would call in and offer to operate for nothing more than a few minutes attention on the national news.

Again, alert the press. Make a lot of noise. Touch up your x-rays to make that ruptured spleen look even worse than it really is and sell them to the National Enquirer. Contact foreign news outlets and send the story worldwide so they can mock us in places like Indonesia and Pakistan where they have national health care and a humanitarian outlook.

Nothing bad will happen to you. Nothing bad can happen to you because you're old; old people have nothing to fear, not even fear itself.

Same with housing. You're old and you don't live in a slum but you hope to move into one as soon as you can afford it? Say no more. Camp out in the lobby of City Hall. Pitch a tent on the lawn. Surround yourself with a lot of other fragile old-timers and summon the press to announce your demands. Threaten to keel over dead if they won't listen and introduce them to your attorney who'll sue their ass for murdering a homeless and broken senior citizen.

Folks, every one of the actions outlined above is a valid protest against the inhumanity of man and the callous indifference of a political system designed solely to maintain the status quo. Insist on your rights both as citizens and members of the human race. You've earned the right to an even break and you won't settle for less, by God.

Once you've eaten, had your operation, and found a decent place to stay, hie yourself down to the polling booth and start making changes by voting the bastards out in wholesale lots. That'll get their attention!

Survival Rules
1. If you're old, broke, and hungry learn to steal.
2. Steal selectively, no luxuries.
3. Steal enough and no more.
4. Assume a proud mien when caught. You're not the one who should be ashamed.
5. Demand a jury trial with TV coverage.
6. Work the same dodge for health care and housing.
7. To bring about meaningful improvements remember our cardinal rule: Vote against every incumbent!

CHAPTER TWENTY-THREE

Anti-Aging Tactics

We do live in remarkable times. Science performs daily miracles, not the phony kind seen only by ignorant peasants or children, but real ones you can see and even replicate. Computers are miracles, and so are TV and atomic bombs and electric motors and rockets and plastic and x-ray machines and heart transplants and a thousand other things in our everyday world.

Can they perform still another miracle and increase our lifespan by a decade or two? Are there already gadgets or herbs or drugs that will slow the aging process and help us live longer and better lives?

Of course there are. Everybody's heard of that doctor in Europe who injected old duffers with cells from sheep gonads and knocked years off their lives. People went to his resort from around the world and paid exorbitant sums because they didn't want to grow old and die. Who can blame them?

Does the stuff work? The doctor said it does and so do some of the people who went there. I've seen testimonial letters from old codgers who claimed the procedure took years off their lives and put a bounce in their step that hadn't been there since World War II. They reported improved skin tone and more stamina and a cheerier outlook after shooting up with the good doctor's gonad cells.

Is it worth a try? Sure, if you've got the money. If you're on your last legs and feel Grim breathing down your neck, why not go for it? What's the worst that can happen? It won't work? So?

What about gadgets like Reich's famous orgone accumulator box where a form of energy called orgone is used to recharge the recipient's batteries? Remember how it works? You sit in the thing and it captures energy out of the air and you soak the stuff up through your pores. It's supposed to increase longevity and improve your health even as it enriches its inventor.

Does this work? Who knows? The point is you're losing that footrace with Grim so what more can you lose? If you can find one of these devices, sign up for a treatment or two. Again, if it works you're in good shape and if it doesn't you're no worse off than you would have been in any case.

Can voodoo help? Some say it can. Practitioners swear they can stop Grim cold with a few chicken parts, some magic potions, a lucky amulet or two, and lots of wild, very erotic dancing around fires late at night. If you know any voodooists, give it a try. You'll enjoy the dancing part and enough bizarre stuff will go on to convince you that something sure as hell happened to you.

Watch out for the curses, though. If you manage to offend the voodoo guy, like by not offering enough money for the services rendered, he might slap a curse on you and make your life a living hell. You could even get the old doll and pins routine and really be in for it.

And don't be fooled by voodooists who offer to revive you after you've died and been buried for a time. Everybody knows these guys are talking about zombies and you don't want that. You'd end up with mobs of enraged villagers chasing you through the fields with torches and sharpened stakes to drive through your heart.

You've got to be careful in your quest for longevity. Avoid guys with fangs and wearing black capes. They'll promise eternal life in exchange for a nip at your neck and turn you into a vampire in the process. Vampires do live forever, as we know, but is that a life? They can't stand daylight or even see themselves in a mirror, and the mere sight of a cross discombobulates them completely. All in all, I think you can pass on the vampire bit.

How about cryogenics? You know, where they freeze your carcass after death and keep the thing on ice while waiting for someone to find a cure for whatever it was that killed you. Is this a viable idea?

Nobody knows yet because so far nobody's been revived to see if it works. It looks good on paper, though. We know stuff can be frozen and kept fresh for years, even centuries. Remember that guy they found in the Alps a while back? The one wearing the leather suit? They claim he was frozen in the ice for five thousand years and he was almost as good as new. Of course, they didn't revive him but he looked pretty good considering how long he'd been dead.

If you've got lots of money maybe you should spend some on a freezer plan. It's true it may never work but you won't know it if it doesn't and it could make a hell of a difference if it does. Give the cryogenics people a call and set it up. Alert them as you're breathing your last and they can rush a freezer over by express mail. Your friends will probably scoff and mock you but you'll get the last laugh if it works.

I understand there's a new wrinkle in this cryogenics business, by the way. Proponents claim it has a real chance of working but there's a catch. The candidate has to be frozen while in reasonably good health; that is, he must be alive at the time. The idea is that freezing living matter is much more likely to keep all the parts intact than waiting until the customer is dead. I think they call that murder, though, so you might want to pass on that one.

In any case, this poses certain moral and legal problems. Is it okay to knock a guy off in order to save his life at some future time? And would the guy who does the knocking off be charged with murder? Still another problem is finding people in reasonably good health who are willing to die in the hope they'll live again. Personally, I think a bird in hand is the operative condition here.

Incidentally, didn't they freeze dry Ted Williams recently? Even if he does come back he'll just be another old man with what—two or three years to live in a convalescent home? Hardly seems worth the trouble.

Is Ponce de Leon's fountain a possibility? Apparently millions of people think so because Florida's filled with old-timers who are looking for it. I've heard the average age in that state is sixty-four and it has a surfeit of people who've passed the century mark. Maybe just being in Florida is close enough to the fabled fountain to do a body some good.

Can there be such a fountain? Actually, it's not likely because if ol' Ponce had found it he'd still be around and he isn't. Even so, with your luck they'd find it right after you've kicked that well-known bucket.

Will science eventually be able to prolong life to the point where people will live to be 150 or more? Maybe, but what good would it do? Women would still run out of sex appeal in their early forties or sooner just as they do now. What woman would much enjoy living a hundred years after she'd exhausted her supply of pheromones?

And what about guys? They wouldn't be able to get it up after eighty and they'd have to live seventy more years with all the virility of a eunuch after prostate surgery. What's the point?

Besides, it doesn't matter in the end, does it? So you go in for regularly scheduled transplants and ingest sheep gonads by the pound and climb in and out of deep freezes and dance with voodooists and it's all for naught at last.

Grim eventually gets you. You can fend him off, fight a delaying action, trick him by moving around a lot, use pseudonyms, bob and weave all you like and one day your name will pop up on his computer screen and Grim will arrive with scythe in hand and cut you down like a shock of wheat in some farmer's field.

And then where'll you be? Dead, that's where.

The stoics were right; don't worry about it. Live as long as you can as gracefully as you can and then greet Grim with a ready grin and get along to whatever comes next.

Survival Rules
1. Buy an orgone accumulator box for your rec room.
2. Consider voodoo but pass on the zombie bit.
3. Avoid guys with fangs and black capes.
4. Sign up for a freezer plan.
5. Move to Florida and look for Ponce's fountain.
6. Or just relax. What the hell, we're all dead in the end, anyway.

CHAPTER TWENTY-FOUR

Drugs/Booze and Sobriety

Nancy Reagan's famous dictum against drugs has apparently fallen on deaf ears. Every time you turn around you read where the feds have seized another shipload of cocaine or rounded up an international marijuana smuggling outfit somewhere. If people were saying no there'd be no market for all this stuff and they'd have to shut down the Drug Enforcement Agency and allied groups that depend on an active drug trade to stay in business.

Oh, we have made progress, of course. Just ask the drug czar. Why, to hear him tell it he's pretty much cleaned up the drug trade and is ready to move on to more challenging work. Isn't that hilarious?

Still, what do these drug wars have to do with our senior citizens? How many eighty-year-old dope smokers are out there? The answer is more than you think and not enough. I read recently where pot use is rising amongst Boomers because they know about it from their misspent youth and so are returning to its comforting arms. It's another sign of the sort of wisdom that comes with advanced age.

The fact is our drug czars have lied to us and so have all politicians and cops and Bible-thumpers and the DARE people and the media and everybody else with access to ink or something electronic. They've told us marijuana is the Devil's work, that pot smoking is a sin and a sure route to hell's fiery furnaces. All nonsense, of course.

Marijuana is actually good medicine and useful as a specific for many health problems. I myself have used pot every day for thirty-seven years to counter the effects of glaucoma and I know it's worked at least half the time because I can still see out of one eye.

I know many others that have used pot for a wide range of ailments and all agree the stuff works wonders. We now have thirteen states that have passed medical marijuana laws to allow patients to obtain and use marijuana and more will likely follow suit in coming elections.

What's more, marijuana is especially good for Boomers as they have more health problems than do Gen-Xers and pot can cure almost everything except actual death. And even that's not certain. Remember Lazarus in the Bible? How he rose from the dead? Well, a recent study by Middle East scholars found that Lazarus' tomb was near a field of burning marijuana plants and it was the pot smoke that leaked into his lungs and jump-started his heart.

Some think this story may be apocryphal; others hint that Lazarus himself may be apocryphal but we can't go into that here.

For more on this subject, see my book Grandpa's Marijuana Handbook and/or the video/DVD titled Grandpa's Marijuana Handbook (the movie).

But even if marijuana's okay that doesn't mean some of that other stuff isn't dangerous. Cocaine and heroin and uppers and downers and similar heavy-duty drugs are to be avoided by everybody and especially seniors. Nobody mucked about with any of that stuff back in the fifties; our bodies were tabernacles back then and we were damn careful about what we put into them.

Of course, we smoked cigarettes; everybody smoked cigarettes. Ball players, movie stars, even doctors were smokers. Ronald Reagan posed for Camel ads and lured countless young people into the smokers' fold. We called them coffin nails and they were, too. The things shorted out hearts and clogged arteries and drove a lot of us to early graves.

What's that? Prohibition? Oh, sure, we all drank now and then. Back in the '20s blind pigs were the centers of our social lives. Bootleggers were selling booze on every corner and everybody had a flask in his pocket at the football stadium on Saturday. It was illegal, of course, but nobody worried much about that.

Surely, you can't draw any parallel between bootlegging booze and selling drugs, though. Everybody drinks booze and only crazed addicts use drugs. You can see the difference in the sentences handed down for both crimes. Bootleggers used to draw six-month sentences in the workhouse while cocaine sellers get life without parole. That ought to tell you something.

So America's oldsters come out foursquare against all harmful drugs and would actively support the government's war on drugs if there were the slightest chance of them ever winning it. Why is it everybody in the world knows the fed's have lost the war except our leaders?

Besides, it costs too much. The feds, et al., spend billions on the drug war, jail countless thousands and wreak great harm on innocent victims, seize property without due process, conduct random searches at will, kick in doors at midnight and terrorize the occupants on patently absurd suspicions, and all this madness and mayhem never makes the slightest dent in our drug culture.

So let's surrender and spend some of that money on care for America's old-timers.

But if cocaine is verboten, booze is still okay. Three or four cocktails of an evening can make life worthwhile. After all, a person has to unwind after a hard day and if a few ounces of Scotch helps where's the harm? It's not like it's illegal, you know.

They say, though, that a lot of our kids are starting to drink more these days. A lot of them drink to excess, in fact, and a lot of them drink and drive and we all know what that means. Still, we should be thankful that our kids are drinking and not doing drugs.

And while we're strongly anti-drugs, we're not against stuff like Valium and other prescription drugs. Everybody knows there's a big difference between street drugs and the ones we get from doctors. We can trust our doctors, you know, and rely on them to make sure we only get hooked on approved drugs that have been clinically tested and manufactured under close government supervision.

But doesn't Valium alter the mind, some might ask. Maybe it does but it's not like heroin or cocaine, is it? Valium only gives a person a little buzz, that's all, sort of like marijuana, in fact. It relaxes people and makes them feel good and there's nothing wrong with feeling good is there?

Some might even argue that advanced age is a time when we might want to kind of mellow out, as it were. When ancient Romans got old it was considered okay to overindulge in wine and spend your days in a kind of happy half-stupor. Maybe they were onto something.

Now, if you're into your eighties and busy running a chicken franchise empire, you may have little spare time for mellowing out, but what if you're just an average Joe who's eighty and looks and feels it. Your day consists of watching TV and risking little walks to the local 7-Eleven to socialize with the other old geezers who hang out there. Life has left you in the lurch, nudged you aside and filled your place with some kid a third your age.

Astonishing.

So maybe a little mind-altering is called for. If the real world has rejected you, maybe it's not such a bad idea to move on to another world, one of your own making where old-timers can find a little solace while waiting for a somewhat tardy Grim to round them up. Does it make a hell of a lot of difference now?

A little pot of an evening will make a bad sitcom funnier or a soap almost make sense. Or you might consider ordering in some vodka or Scotch or a flagon of wine and pouring yourself a wee drop now and again. It'll do wonders for your frame of mind and overall mental health.

You could invite friends in and make it an event. Ring up some other old biddies in nearby units and announce you're having a party. Bang on the doors of any widowers in the vicinity and insist they stop by. Tell them you'd like a strong man around because two or three of the prettier widows will likely get carried away and start taking off their clothes. Any old sap will fall for that story, even one who's ninety and hasn't had it up in a decade.

Make up a bowl of punch for any non-drinkers and spike it with a fifth of gin so they won't feel left out. After a few drinks when everybody's loosened up, try to start something with the ladies. You guys can pinch a derriere or cop a feel when you get the chance. Ladies can loose a barrage of pheromones if they have any left and flash a lot of nylon-clad thigh and eye-opening cleavage to add another element to the affair.

If done right your unit could become a kind of salon similar to those that flourished in Europe in the late-eighteenth century. All the high muck-a-mucks in the place will vie for an invitation to your soirees and you'll be the toast of the geriatric set.

But could all this booze be a problem? Wouldn't it hurt your health, lead to strokes or worse? What about becoming an alcoholic and ending up on skid row or driving drunk and causing an accident?

Good questions. Let's look at them. Driving? You don't drive anymore. The cops seized your license when your doctor blew the whistle on you and told them your were legally blind. In fact, you can't even find the car now. What's more, nobody else drives in your condo, either.

Alcoholism? Easy. Never drink before dark. That way, you can let demon rum and your neighbors know who's in charge. Will the booze harm your health? What health? You're a senior citizen, for God's sake. Grim is in the neighborhood; he may be just around the corner or even reaching for your doorbell at this very minute. I say again, what have you got to lose?

Or if you don't like booze try some of the many prescription items available through your family doctor. Call him up and tell him you're nervous and hyper lately and need something to even you out, as it were. Suggest a hundred Valium tabs for starters and pop a few of them with breakfast. You'll be amazed at how they'll smooth out your day and give you a whole new outlook on life.

Why, I've known people who went from crabby, grouchy old fools to cheery, pleasant people everybody loved and esteemed, and they did it by recharging their synapses courtesy of the pharmaceutical industry. Not only were their own lives made better; so were those of the people around them.

Science has done wonders in recent years and it's foolish not to take advantage of its success. There are worse things in this tired old world than altering your mind just a shade and taking a close look at things from a slightly different angle. So just say no to sobriety and add a bit of novelty to your life.

And isn't that salon idea an intriguing one?

Survival Rules
1. Just say no to all drugs except marijuana.
2. Remember the Romans and that happy half stupor.
3. Stock up on chemicals from your pharmacist and create a world of your own.
4. Establish that salon.
5. Remember, you have nothing to lose as Grim was seen in the vicinity just a few minutes ago.

CHAPTER TWENTY-FIVE

Wills

Okay, so we're getting close to the end of the trail here, close enough that we should devote some time to wills and inheritances and estates and heirs. Is there anything special we should know about this stuff? Can we work it to our advantage? What if we have heirs and nothing to leave them?

Start by making a will. Even if you're poor as a church mouse, make a will and let everybody know you've got one. If you don't have any money to hire a lawyer, pick up some forms in an office supply store and fill them out. Just having a will adds a certain cachet to any man's life and makes him all the more appealing to others, especially potential heirs.

Don't tell people what's in your will, though. Keeping everybody guessing is how you make a will pay off while you're still among the living. Suppose you're the average old-timer and you're broke. You have a meager pension and a few paltry stocks and live on canned dog food almost exclusively. You have potential heirs, too.

Hint that you're loaded. Tell your shiftless kids that your old prospector buddy from the Klondike died and left you half of his valuable gold mine. It's tied up in litigation by some scurrilous claim jumping lawyers in Anchorage, but you'll soon have clear title and a vast fortune.

Inform them that you've drawn up a new will

and watch them scurry around vying for your favor. You'll be invited to dinner regularly and nieces and nephews you haven't seen in decades will lavish attention and even affection on you and remark how they've always regarded you as their favorite uncle/aunt. They'll take you for scenic drives in the country, supply you with fresh cigars, ply you with gifts, and generally do their level best to win you over in hopes of being remembered in your will.

What's more, your love life will improve dramatically. Every widow in town will move in on you like Huns overrunning Rome. You'll be romanced as never before. Widows are drawn to rich old guys like iron filings to a magnet and will do anything to win their hand in matrimony holy or otherwise. With any luck at all you'll be able to score at will and add a new dimension to an otherwise dreary old age.

Another caveat, though. Since all these people can only succeed after you're dead, it behooves you to watch them lest they decide to help things along and dispatch you themselves. Be alert. Did the brakes on your car fail? Suspect tampering. Drive-by shooters spray your house with Uzis? Check your no-good nephew's alibi.

Your house catches fire? You suffer food poisoning? A mail bomb blows your elbow off? These and similar goings on might indicate that one or more of your heirs is trying to kill you and you'll have to take precautions. Don't trust any of them. Stay away from cliffs. Don't go sailing with an heir. Hire a food taster. Always sit with your back against the wall.

You can neutralize them somewhat if you're clever. Have a printer print up a bunch of phony stock certificates. Make them look like blue chippers, IBM and ATT and GE and good utilities. Arrange them in piles. Invite different heirs to your place and show them these piles of stocks and announce that you're leaving them some. Riffle them like cards and hint that you suspect certain other heirs are out to get you and enlist them to help you expose the culprits.

They'll believe their fortune is made and willingly do your bidding to stay in your good graces. You can play one against the rest and keep them all off balance with this scheme. Remember, all's fair in love and war and the duping of heirs.

The point of all this is that people respect people with money—or people they think have money—and their respect diminishes in direct proportion to one's increasing poverty. Presidents and kings fawn over billionaires; homeless people are scorned by yellow dogs. If you don't have money pretend you do and you acquire respect on the spot. It isn't necessary to display wealth, either. If you had to show up in a Rolls Royce or live in a mansion you'd be hard pressed to make the scheme work. Assume an eccentric air. Hint that you're very wealthy but disdain worldly things. Tell them you're a devotee of Thoreau and you've learned to simplify, simplify. They're greedy and will buy it every time.

On the other side of this coin, don't waste any time worrying about being included in other people's wills because you're so old you don't have a chance of outliving a chipmunk let alone some rich guy with a staff of MDs on his payroll. Working the will dodge is a game for young people who can wait for somebody to die.

Incidentally, women are very successful at the will scam. It's easy for a slim young thing to hornswoggle some old fool into marrying her and placing her first in line for a swipe at his assets when he goes. What's more, a really determined slim young thing can—and often does—hurry the old codger along by laying waste to his brains via excess sex and thereby destroying what's left of his health. This is actually easier to do than you'd think since these old fools rarely have any brains to begin with or they'd never marry such women.

Can young guys marry rich women and do the same thing? No, because rich old women hardly ever die. You could marry a rich widow of seventy-five and next thing you know Willard Scott would be honoring her on her 104th birthday and you'd be in a nursing home yourself.

And there you have it. You take my advice and work the will dodge on your unsuspecting heirs and you'll improve the quality of your old age by leaps and bounds. It could be the difference between a life of comfort and ease and life in a cardboard box on Main Street, U.S.A. I urge you to opt for the former.

Survival Rules

1. Make a will even if you're flat broke. It looks good.

2. If you don't have any money, lie.
3. Play your heirs against each other.
4. They'll probably try to kill you. Watch them.
5. Be eccentric to cover your inability to display wealth.
6. Widows: Marry rich widowers and outlast them.
7. Widowers: Avoid slim young things or risk having your brains fucked out.

CHAPTER TWENTY-SIX

Old Folks' Homes

Let's face it, if you live long enough you'll come to be regarded as a nuisance and all around pain in the neck and somebody will try to put you in an old folks' home to get you out of the way. What to do about it?

First, be on your guard. It usually begins when somebody (an heir) shows up with some papers for you to sign.

"Yeah, just sign right here, Dad," your Gen-Xer kid will say. "It's just a legal formality, nothing important. You won't need to bother reading it."

The papers will be written in Latin and covered all over with seals, ribbons, and stamps and come with multiple copies. There will probably be two or three strangers standing nearby including a notary public and the required witnesses necessary to make the documents legal and binding for all eternity. Your heir will be smiling.

He'll try to catch you at a weak moment, too, in hopes of taking you unawares. This guy will show up as they're wheeling your carcass out of the operating room after gall bladder surgery and try to thrust a pen in your hand before you come out of the anesthesia or nail you the day after a cerebral hemorrhage when you're unable to think clearly.

Don't fall for this trick. Refuse to sign anything without your lawyer's okay. The documents are probably commitment papers consigning you to perpetual care at the Sunny Dale Convalescent Home where no one has ever convalesced enough to get well and go home. Put your John Hancock on the dotted line and you'll never taste freedom again.

Okay, but what if this guy does manage to catch you right after your stroke and you sign the papers and end up at Sunny Dale. What then?

It's the end of the trail then, that's what it is. As soon as they get you inside and out of sight of the officials for the Society for the Prevention of Cruelty to Old People, they'll cart your corpus to a ward full of other old-timers similarly afflicted and consign you into the maws of this country's equivalent of the Eskimo's famed put-them-on-ice method of handling unwanted old folks and wash their hands of your aged self for good and all.

A word of caution. When you arrive at Sunny Dale it's essential that you don't do anything to attract unwanted attention. See, if the guys in charge decide you're a nuisance and a potential troublemaker, they'll shoot you so full of various chemicals you won't know which end is up from one month to the next. They'll turn you into a geriatric zombie and use you as a doorstop in the rec room and nobody will ever hear a peep out of you again.

The trick is to go along with them at first, gain their confidence and hoodwink them into thinking you love it there. Compliment the management on running a first-rate old folks' home. Offer to inform on other inmates to make points with the staff. Assume a cheery aspect. You want to lull them into a false sense of security so when they relax their guard you can make a break for it.

That's your only out, you know. The Sunny Dales of the world are like black holes that almost nothing escapes from. I say almost because it does happen on occasion that some strong-willed, determined people do get out and resume real living again, but the odds are mighty long, indeed. Still, it's break out or nothing so you have to go for it.

You'll need to organize the other inmates to join you since breaking out will require a team effort if it's to succeed. Meet clandestinely at midnight and lay your plans. Send out scouts to reconnoiter the grounds and find the weak points in their security system such as breaks in the wall or holes in the fence or alarm locations or the routines of the armed guards so you'll know the best routes to the outside. Get blueprints and maps of the buildings and grounds and coordinate them for future reference. Stockpile ropes, emergency rations, ladders, flashlights, pith helmets, a compass, and similar materiel you'll need for a successful escape.

Try to recruit members who have the best chance of making a clean getaway. You can do that by restricting the escape party to those less than ninety and demanding that all successful applicants be ambulatory to a greater or lesser degree. If you can find people with previous experience escaping from things so much the better.

Hold dry runs. Practice scaling high walls and rappelling down the sides of tall buildings while wearing full escape packs. Hold ladder drills and knot-tying sessions and first-aid practice. In other words, devote your full time to getting the hell out of Sunny Dale and back to the real world where people can live like real people instead of a bunch of societal rejects with nothing better to do than sit around waiting for Grim to show up with their names on his computer printouts.

You'll notice a recurring problem with your escape party if you wait too long to make your move, i.e., they'll die off on you and need to be replaced periodically. This can't be helped as people in their eighties commonly drop dead unexpectedly in spite of our best efforts to prevent them from doing so. This means you'll have an ongoing recruiting problem and need to be on the lookout for potential new members on a regular basis.

By the way, make it a policy from the start not to attend funerals during your stay at Sunny Dale. Claim you're allergic to the funeral march or flowers or dead people or maudlin enterprises, but don't go or you won't have time for any other activity as the Sunny Dalers of the world tend to die off at an alarming rate. Something as complicated and time consuming as arranging an escape plan will be out of the question if you fall into the trap of attending every funeral that comes along.

Anyway, you should have completed your planning within ninety days or so of your arrival and be ready to make a run for it. When the time comes go all out and don't look back. Storm the gatehouse and overpower the guards, seize the director's car, crash the main gate, and head for the city where you can lose yourself in the crowds.

Once you've escaped remember that you're on your own and dare not see any relatives who may have a stake in your capture and re-incarceration because they'll fink on you every time. As long as you're in Sunny Dale and unable to make trouble, they'll be able to despoil your property and line their own pockets, but if you're running loose in the city you'll be a threat to them and theirs and that will piss them off.

The best thing is to hide out somewhere until the heat wears off. You should probably head for a warm climate in case you end up living on the street for a time while you chart a course of action. Florida is nice and so is Southern California or Arizona. Whatever you do don't light out for places like Minnesota or Montana even though you'll be safe from arrest since nobody would ever guess you'd be stupid enough to go there.

Of course, you'll want to launch legal action to get your commitment reversed and retrieve your fortune and that may require your staying in the neighborhood. In that case you'll have to hole-up somewhere nearby and find a lawyer who'll work on a contingency until you recover your money and can pay him.

The problem here is that good lawyers want their money up front and you don't want the bad ones. You need Ellery Queen and not some half-wit who's cheap but can hardly find his way to the courthouse. Still, you can't fight your heirs' attorneys without one of your own so you'll have to cut some kind of deal even if the best you can do is to hire an Ellery Queen look-alike.

Once you're on your own you can start living again. It's a good idea to keep on the move to throw Grim off your track because as soon as he finds out you've fled Sunny Dale he'll take up the search so he can update his printouts. He can't stop round and pick you up if he doesn't know where the hell you are, can he?

Head for one of those cheap residence hotels that can be found in every city's skid row and get a room. As an old-timer on the loose in modern-day America, you'll be living in penury and be in need of charity to stay alive so see if you can get a place near a soup kitchen and save yourself a long walk three times a day. You'll doubtless want to lay in a supply of dog food, as this appears to be a staple in the diet of many of America's senior citizens.

Once safely ensconced in your seedy hotel room you can begin laying plans to regain your proper place in society even as you get on with the business of living again. If you can still walk, get out and mingle with real people. Enjoy the sunshine if there is any. Make new friends if you can find anyone who'll talk to you. Shoplift rings of bologna and loaves of French bread both as a means of getting something to eat and for the excitement of living on the edge. Remember, you're an old person on the brink of death and they can't—or won't—do anything to you even if they catch you red-handed, as we saw in the chapter on Shoplifting.

In other words, now that you've managed to escape from Sunny Dale you should cram as much living as you can into the time remaining to you before Grim gets a new fix on your current whereabouts and shows up with his cursed printouts. Consider the extra time a gift, your postponed appointment with Grim a reprieve of sorts, and live again while you may.

After all, most people who end up in old folks' homes actually end up there; it's literally the end of the trail for them. You've earned yourself a bonus and you want to make the most of it.

As they say, live dangerously; it's the only time you live at all.

Survival Rules
1. Beware of heirs with papers to be signed. Sign nothing without your lawyer!
2. Don't make a fuss when arriving at the Home or they'll shoot you full of chemicals.
3. Outwit them. Make them think you like it there.
4. Start planning your escape at once.
5. Recruit others but sign up only ambulatory people.
6. Move fast or your team will die off on you.
7. Once out head for a warm climate.
8. Keep moving to throw Grim off your trail.

CHAPTER TWENTY-SEVEN

The Problem of Dead Friends

"Hear about Bill? Dropped dead yesterday."

"No! Bill? I can't believe it! Why, I was talking to him just the other day!"

I don't know why people always profess astonishment that anyone they recently spoke to could possibly have died, but it seems a universal trait since one hears it continually.

"Yep, heart. Went like that." Snaps fingers. "That leaves only you and me and the Frisoli twins from the old neighborhood."

"Bill's dead. I still can't believe it."

"Oh, it's true, all right, they're droppin' like flies, aren't they? Pretty soon there won't be anybody left at all."

You've noticed it, too, I suppose. People you knew, friends, relatives, co-workers, classmates, disappear one by one as Grim catches up to them and ships them into the maw of the netherworld never to be seen again. Isn't that scary, though?

If you manage to stay alive long enough you'll get caught up in this all-my-friends-are-dead syndrome and experience two predictable reactions. The first is that you'll be alarmed for your own mortality since it's plain if everybody you've known has dropped like a fly it means the time is rapidly drawing nigh when you will be one of the flies yourself and that's not a wholesome thought.

The truth is, of course, that the deaths of our contemporaries are tragic mainly because they remind us of our own upcoming deaths, and especially is this so if the one who's passed, croaked, died is a parent. It's almost inconceivable that our parents should die since they're so important to us and so closely tied to our own lives; yet the real anguish comes from the realization that their deaths indicate our own is not far off.

What can you do about this? It may help to have very old parents if that can be arranged. You can help bring this happy condition about by putting them on a vitamin supplement program with lots of vitamin C and carotene and all the rest. Encourage them to exercise regularly but moderately. No running, jogging, rope skipping, calisthenics, or aerobic dancing. And suggest lots of sex, of course.

Load them up with life insurance as people with lots of insurance hardly ever die. See that they have frequent medical checkups. Call each day and remind them to take their medicine. If they live in one of our large cities, have iron bars affixed to their windows to keep out any would-be killers. In other words, keep your parents alive as long as possible and you can fool yourself into thinking your own life will be a bit more secure.

None of this will help ultimately, of course, since Grim's computers are busily computing your own remaining days with unrelenting determination; in other words, you're deluding yourself but that's okay as delusion is often an excellent substitute for reality.

Now to the second part of this equation. What about the deaths of all those friends, classmates, relatives, co-workers, the ones you read about in the obits or hear about from friends or discover accidentally by attending a funeral and finding it's somebody you know—or knew? What about these people and their passing, croaking, dying? Haven't you noticed something peculiar, something both exhilarating and at the same time shameful when you learn of a friend's death?

I'm talking about the vague sense of glee that accompanies each such announcement. Or elation. Or triumph. There's even a word for this feeling, the German schadenfreude, which means a feeling of pleasure caused by another's misfortune. We all experience it from time to time and everyone recognizes it when it shows up.

"Say, you hear about Ed? Died yesterday. A Mack truck got him."

You're truly surprised and shocked and you say so. "Ed? He's dead? Why, I was just talking..."

At the same time you're expressing your dismay at poor Ed's passing you're thinking, "So, you're dead and I'm not! How about that? I'm still extant and you're just ex, period. I win! It looks like I was the better man after all. I outlived you so that means I win, Ed. How about that, eh?"

Confess, isn't that what you're really thinking? Or if not those exact words, then something close, something both exhilarating and shameful? Don't you get a certain perverse pleasure on learning that you've outlived yet another of your comrades? Of course you do, everybody does.

You pore over the obits with uncommon interest, don't you? You study each entry carefully, note peoples' ages and causes of death, catch your breath when you spot a familiar name.

"O'Houlihan?" you gasp. "It is him! Ed O'Houlihan, by God! Age sixty-one. Run over by a Mack truck!" You lower the paper and gaze into the middle distance in a kind of reverie. "So ol' Ed's a goner, is he? Sixty-one. Yep, that's right, Ed was a year younger'n me; he was a junior when I graduated. And now he's a goner and I'm not. How about that?"

You can see others share this peculiar emotion when they gather at the funeral home for the viewing. People enter awkwardly, their eyes drawn to the coffin at the far end of the room even as they themselves are drawn to it. They sign the visitors' log and move to the coffin where they stand and peer down at the late departed.

"Poor Ed. Only sixty-one."

"Looks good, though."

"Yeah."

"I still can't believe it. Why, I was just..."

As they stand peering into the coffin at the unfortunate Ed each stands a little straighter, throws his shoulders back, thrusts out his chest and revels silently in his good fortune to be alive when poor Ed isn't.

People mill about and stand in small groups and make suitable comments about the erstwhile Ed. After a bit talk turns from Ed to other matters and a noisy chatter fills the formerly somber room. Laughter is heard and a party atmosphere begins to manifest itself as Ed is all but forgotten.

Or is he? People sneak occasional glances in Ed's direction from time to time. Some end up gazing thoughtfully at his horizontal form with a vacant look on their mugs. Are they saddened by Ed's departure? Lamenting his loss? Pondering the mysteries of life and death and other worlds and fate?

Hell, no. They're thinking, "Well, by God, you're dead and I'm not, Ed! How 'bout that? I'm a year older'n you and you're dead. I'll probably live till I'm ninety or more and you're dead at sixty-one. How 'bout that?"

Is this a bad thing? Is there some innate evil quality in each of us that causes us to take a macabre delight in the demise of others? Of course not. It's nothing more than a kind of defense mechanism against the terrors of our own deaths.

If you're outliving all your friends and neighbors, isn't that a good thing? Every time somebody else dies it means you didn't because you're still here to attend his funeral or read about it in the obituaries. It means you're a winner in life's race. Grim's misplaced your records, you've been spared by a computer glitch and allowed to race on toward the century mark while the losers are rounded up in their forties, fifties, and sixties.

You're alive! Why not rejoice? Why not celebrate your good luck? Would you feel better about things if you were Ed? Ed's a goner. Kaput. He's no longer extant. Circle his obituary notice in red ink and reflect on your good fortune and his own lack of it. It's only natural to do so.

Believe me, if it were you in that box and Ed was the one signing the visitors' log, he'd be grinning inwardly to beat the band and relishing his own victory over you in our collective footrace with the Grim Reaper.

Wasn't it ever thus?

Survival Rules
1. Our parents' deaths are traumatic so arrange to have very old ones.
2. Have lots of insurance on them as heavily insured people seldom die.
3. Relax. It's normal to view friends' deaths with a sort of subdued glee.
4. Check the obits daily for new sources of glee.
5. Try not to break out in a wide grin while viewing the remains.
6. Outliving your friends means you may never have to die so keep it up.

CHAPTER TWENTY-EIGHT

Suicide

Now we really are closing things out here. The end of that trail is within sight; in fact, it's practically at hand, or soon will be if we get much involved in what Hamlet called self-slaughter.

As everybody knows, this is currently a major issue in America what with people writing books exhorting us all to kill ourselves forthwith and mad scientists running around with death machines doing Grim's work for him. Talk shows are packed with people who are either planning ways to kill their fellows or people looking for ways to be killed. Next, they'll probably have mad scientists doing in clients on live TV while the audience watches with mouths agape.

Let's take a closer look at this suicide business, especially as it applies to old-timers like us. What's it all about? Are we talking murder or just manslaughter? Are death machines desirable? Are there alternatives? What are the moral implications? Legal ones?

It's okay for most people to speculate about suicide because they're in robust health and can approach the subject dispassionately, but people in their eighties are considerably more likely to be faced with much different circumstances.

But let's start with the history of suicide and see where we've been before we look to see where we want to go. For openers, suicide has always been very popular everywhere except in Catholic countries where it's forbidden by executive fiat, as it were.

Early men killed themselves in droves in order to placate non-existent gods or on orders of the headman who needed something spectacular to entertain his restless subjects. Egyptians held asps to their breasts. Ancient Greeks cheerfully threw themselves from precipices and Romans slit their wrists in tubs of warm water or hurled their bodies on swords held by trusted lieutenants.

Apparently, everyone approved of such antics, as you never read where anyone demurred. It was more or less assumed that these people had every right to dispatch themselves at their own discretion. It didn't become a moral issue until the Catholic Church rose into its ascendancy and laid down a new set of rules.

According to Catholics, suicide is an immoral act and absolutely forbidden by canon law, which could be backed up by cannons of another sort if challenged. In fact, suicides were even forbidden burial in so-called consecrated ground where people of a more decent sort were laid to rest.

Of course, there were exceptions, as there always are in matters like this. Heroes who sacrificed their lives for the good of the country, or especially the Church, were quite another matter altogether. Such people were obviously of a different stripe and entitled to different rules.

When Colin Kelly flew his bomber into a Japanese warship at the beginning of World War II he was an instant hero and martyr. The fact is he killed himself.

It was a clear-cut case of suicide and everybody knew it, but nobody discussed his act in those terms. Kelly was a national hero, justifiably so, and that's how we saw him.

So it appears that the subject isn't as cut and dried as we might imagine. It would seem there are suicides and suicides and only highly trained religiosos can tell the difference between good ones and bad ones. Even worse, religiosos differ among themselves. Most Protestants readily accept suicide and say naught against it. In some cases, many Protestants even encourage it as they have with the Rev. Swaggart, et al.

So right away a potential suicide is faced with a dilemma. If a Catholic is determined to do himself in, should he convert to a Protestant faith that allows suicide? (Yes, by all means. Why take chances?)

In brief, then, it appears that the right or wrong of suicide is pretty much a matter of individual conscience. People approve it or not according to their upbringing and training without recourse to any sort of rational considerations. This isn't surprising since people organize their lives along such lines most of the time anyway, of course.

So is suicide moral or not? Your guess is as good as anyone else's.

Is it legal? Depends. Some states have laws against it and threaten to prosecute any would-be suicides that fail and are around to answer for their "crime." In truth, though, you never actually hear where a state has prosecuted a failed suicide since such an act would be totally stupid and punishment unenforceable.

What would they do to such a guy? Fine him? Wouldn't he just pay the fine and then leap in front of a bus? Or could they jail him? To what avail? There are lots of ways to do yourself in even in prison. Besides, would any sentence mean anything to a guy who was trying to kill himself?

It's safe to say that you may shoot, stab, hang, garrote, poison, and/or defenestrate yourself without fear of being arrested. At worst they'll subject you to scrutiny by a shrink before letting you go.

Okay, so suicide is moral if you think it is and more or less legal. That should help all the ethicists and legal worrywarts out there decide whether it's for them or not. It seems such people can safely ignore these factors and concentrate on others like how best to do it and what the results are likely to be.

Now the question is should people be committing suicide at all? What are some acceptable reasons for it? Are there any guidelines? Are there people who've experienced suicide first-hand and can advise us on its subtleties and nuances? How, exactly, does one go about it? Are there any hidden dangers?

First, the reasons. Some people commit suicide because their girl dumped them or they're unable to lose weight or they got fired. These are not good reasons. Guys can find new girls, as there's an unlimited supply of them around. Fat people, by all accounts, are supposed to be jolly and fun loving and hence have no business killing themselves. As for jobs, I can think of damn few I'd kill myself over.

No, most agree that suicide is not the answer for everyday problems that affect everyone. If people start killing themselves willy-nilly we'll soon have a shortage of people and have to encourage immigration from Mexico and the Far East and nobody wants that. Life is a challenge and we have a duty to put up a good fight before being overtaken in Grim's implacable pursuit.

Then is there one universally recognized reason for doing oneself in, some unutterable condition that is always a sufficient reason for taking the gas pipe? There is and that unutterable condition is failed health.

Life can be intolerable without good health, or at least adequate health. Colds are okay and so are hangnails, baldness, post-nasal drip, and liver spots. It's even okay for a lot of people who have much more severe afflictions and still find pleasure in being alive. People are in wheelchairs and bedridden and worse and still relish life and long to hear from Willard Scott when their hundredth birthday rolls around.

No one is suggesting suicide for such people, but there are others who are terminally ill and in great pain. Or they're paralyzed or in some way reduced to living less than adequate lives and they do wish to end it all. Freud himself, suffering from oral cancer, said to his doctor, "Let's put an end to this thing." And they did.

Certainly, these people have the right to kill themselves. Whose business could it possibly be except your own? What so-called moralist or dim-witted legislator would have the nerve to suggest they be required to go on living against their will?

Okay, so we've established that suicide is a pro-choice affair and that people in ill health often choose it. Now what about old people specifically? Aren't all too many old-timers in ill health? Aren't ill health and old age almost synonymous?

The fact is there are thousands if not millions of old-timers in this country who are both old and sick. Who would gainsay these folks moving on to a better world just a bit earlier than scheduled? Grim can deal with it. It just means an adjustment on his computer, the hitting of a few keys and the early departure is factored in and life—or death—goes on as before.

We conclude, then, that everyone, and most especially old people, have an absolute right to end their lives whenever the hell they elect to do so. It's nobody else's business. If you're eighty or so, in pain from any source and want to end it all, go ahead and do it. Again, what have you got to lose? Even if you hang in there for another six months or a year or two you only delay the inevitable momentarily.

Well and good. Now we come to the how of things. You're old and broke and tired and afflicted with some dreadful illness that's not, unfortunately, going to be fatal any time soon. Your children have tricked you into signing over all your assets and are arranging to toss your aged corpus into a convenient old folks' home because they don't want you around anymore. All your friends are dead or missing. You haven't got it up in years and aren't likely to in the foreseeable future. So you decide to end it all.

Okay, how? What are your options? Remember, you want to be sure you do it right lest you botch the job and wind up even worse off than you were before. How about a gun then? Everybody knows guns are lethal as hell. Remember how well one worked for Hemingway? Get a gun, one with a large caliber, as large caliber guns are more lethal than smaller ones. A .357 magnum will kill you and two or three friends at the same time if they align themselves properly. It'd be cheaper, too, as you could make a single bullet do the work of three or four.

Are there any drawbacks to guns? Sure, they're messy. That .357 magnum will make a large hole in the wall after making one in your head and somebody will have to re-plaster. There'll also be assorted debris to clean up. The noise may startle your neighbors. And what if you miss?

Suppose your hand jerks at the last moment? You could just graze yourself and survive and look like an idiot who couldn't even manage to shoot himself properly. Wouldn't that be embarrassing?

No, guns are out. What about hanging? Rope's cheap. You could probably buy enough stout Manila hemp to pull off a first-rate hanging for ten bucks. Rope and a bucket to stand on—and kick at the proper moment—and some notebook paper for a suicide note and you're not out more than a few bucks total.

Get a Boy Scout handbook to learn how to tie a decent hangman's knot. You might want to get a black hood to lend a professional touch to the proceedings. Attach the note to your chest, toss the rope over a girder, mount the bucket, and kick 'er away. It's simple.

Drawbacks? Lots of them. For one thing, all this activity with buckets and ropes and knot-tying and handbook research could be tiring and poop an old-timer out before he got to the kicking part. Hanging requires a certain amount of dexterity and even skill and your average octogenarian might not be up to it. Many a would-be elderly suicide has been found fast asleep in a tangle of rope with half-tied hangman's knots and an unfinished note in hand. The poor guy just pooped out, that's all.

You could screw it up and look foolish. One old guy tried hanging himself from a ten-foot high tree branch with a fifteen-foot rope. He was found sitting on the ground with five feet of excess rope draped around him and the poor sap was a laughingstock for years afterwards.

Incredible.

Besides, few of us could do the job right and instead of neatly breaking our neck and rendering ourselves unconscious we'd choke to death and that would be unpleasant to say the least. So let's skip hanging.

Okay, defenestration. We throw ourselves from a window. This is even cheaper than hanging since all that's required is an open window and a straight drop unhindered by open awnings or other impediments to our fall. It's also reliable if we make sure to use a high enough window.

Drawbacks? We might land on somebody below, most likely somebody who wasn't planning to die himself just then, and that would be inappropriate. And then there's the mess again. Somebody would have to clean up after us and that's not acceptable, either. And what if we change our mind halfway down? Wouldn't we feel like a real dope then?

I say no window jumping. I'm afraid of heights, anyway, and see no sense in being terrified in the few seconds I have left en route to terra firma.

So that's no guns, ropes, or windows. What about slashing the wrists? Far too messy. Starving your self? No, the hunger would be unbearable. Eating yourself to death? Umm, possibly. Self-immolation? Are you nuts?! Drowning? No way. A single car accident? No, the air bag would save you.

Ah, I have it! How about the time-honored and much desired death by way of excessive sex? All you have to do is find some sweet young thing—or well-hung young stud depending on your particular sexual persuasion—and get laid repeatedly until the old ticker gives out. Why, this'll kill most old-timers over a long weekend and the rest within a fortnight at most.

And what a way to go! You'll be the envy of your peers; indeed, of people everywhere who hear about it.

"Coopersmith's dead, you know."
"Yeah, I know. They say too much sex killed him."
"Yeah. He always was a lucky bastard."
Shakes head. "What a way to go!"
"Yeah."

TV shows would film your story. They'd do a piece on you in the AARP journal and you'd be asked to speak to other old codgers to tell them how you did it. It could be the biggest thing in your whole life and serve as an example to an entire nation of elderly people who desperately need role models.

Drawbacks? The chief one is you have to be able not only to get it up but keep it up long enough to exhaust yourself and induce death. Since most guys in their eighties can't get the thing even as far as half-staff it might be beyond them. Women, of course, have the advantage again and could easily pull it off if they could just find somebody willing to accommodate them, but that's not an easy task if they're old and bereft of pheromones.

On the whole, then, this won't work for most old people. So what's left? Poison, that's what. Arsenic. Rat bane. Wood alcohol. Barbiturates. Strychnine. Lye. Ptomaine. Carbon monoxide. Any or all of these substances will dispatch you to the next world in a trice and do so neatly and with little fuss or bother.

Take strychnine, for example. This is a favorite of spies and Nazis who made a practice of keeping a poison pill handy in case they were caught and threatened with hanging or worse. You just pop the thing in your mouth and presto! You're deader than a mackerel just like that.

But where do you find a poison pill? Most doctors won't prescribe them unless you can come up with a good reason for needing one without admitting you're planning to kill either yourself or someone else. Local pharmacies don't sell them. About your only hope of getting one is if you happen to know any former spies or Nazis who might have a spare.

Arsenic is readily available, though. Lots of household poisons contain arsenic. Various insect sprays are loaded with the stuff and it's used in rat poisons, too. Drink a glass or two of your ant spray and the chances are you'll be well launched on that ultimate journey.

The same with sleeping pills that contain barbiturates. Mix half-a-pound of them into your tomato juice and you're a goner every time. A can of lye will do the same. So will moonshine that's laced with more than the prescribed amount of wood alcohol.

Another caveat, though. Poisons can be rough on the throat and gastrointestinal tract. Some of them will burn for days before doing the job. Lye, for example, is one to be avoided. Others may leave you in a coma. Still others taste bad. You'll want to do some research as to the specific effects of each before deciding on one.

A favorite is old reliable carbon monoxide. You can do the job for the cost of half a tank of gasoline for the car. Just close the garage up tight, turn on the car, and relax with some coffee and a cruller. The fumes are odorless, tasteless, and lethal. You will, as they say, never know what hit you.

But have a care with carbon monoxide. The stuff can seep into the house and you could end up asphyxiating everybody in the place and any casual visitors who happened by.

One final thing. What about a note? Should you leave one or is it better if you don't? I vote for a note. For one thing a suicide note lets people know what happened so the cops won't think there was foul play and arrest somebody on murder charges. Be sure the note's handwritten, though, or your killer could have written a typed note that would prove useless in establishing suicide. Whatever you do don't make up a note from words cut from a newspaper, as the cops will surely view such a note with suspicion.

Also, try to think of something original to say. Aim for brevity and style. Try for wit, wry humor. Be sure you spell things right and check the grammar as you don't want to appear to be an ignorant blockhead in the last bit of writing you ever do. Write legibly as few things are as irksome as trying to read illegible suicide notes. Use good quality notepaper to show you still have some class and be sure to sign it. Leave it where it can be readily found.

These are just a few suggestions you may find useful. Any creative person could come up with lots more that might better suit his individual preferences. I guess the idea is to keep your eye on the goal and choose something that gets you there with the least fuss and inconvenience.

Well, that's about it. You'll look long and hard to find a more thorough and yet succinct discussion of the pros and cons of suicide in any language anywhere. I know it'll stand you in good stead.

Remember, it's your affair and yours alone. If anyone tells you differently, refer him to me.

Unbelievable.

Non-Survival Rules

1. Suicide is a time-honored practice with the weight of centuries behind it.
2. It's moral if you think it is and legal everywhere.
3. If your religion forbids it, convert to one that approves as a precaution.
4. Suicide is always acceptable when it's a selfless act.
5. Poor health is always a valid reason for doing yourself in.
6. Avoid guns, windows, ropes, slashing, starving, drowning, fire, and similar unpleasant means.
7. If you can swing it opt for death by excessive sex.
8. Poisons are good, especially carbon monoxide, but check them out first.
9. Always leave a note, as a cleverly written note is a nice touch and shows you care.

CHAPTER TWENTY-NINE

Last Words

Most people never even think about their last words until the moment arrives when they need some and then they're forced to ad lib something as Grim comes through the door and you get a lot of pretty poor quality pronouncements as a result. It's far wiser to plan ahead and have something dramatic, something memorable to say when the need arises.

There are some tricks to last words, things you need to know if you're going to go out with some flair. For one thing, you need to make sure there are people around to record what you say and report it to the world at large. It does no good at all to make the most remarkable statement of the decade if there's no one nearby to write it down.

There are rumors, for instance, that when Jim Bowie stood defiantly before hordes of advancing Mexican soldiers at the Alamo he shouted a phrase of such weight and profundity that the Mexicans actually reeled under the force of the words even though none of them understood English. Regrettably, the Mexicans regrouped and shot Bowie deader than a mackerel and left nary a survivor to tell us what it was Bowie said.

Don't let that happen to you. Make it a point to have several reliable witnesses nearby at all times when Grim has been spotted heading your way. It's a good idea to include a minister or, better yet, a bishop amongst the witnesses for their credibility. You might want to have paper and pen handy, too, in case you have a lot of last words and people want to write them down to ensure accuracy.

Accuracy is important, you know. Suppose somebody had mistakenly quoted John Paul Jones as crying out, "I will not give up!" instead of the more memorable, "I have not yet begun to fight!" See the difference? The drama is missing in the former; there's no sense of the moment, no sense of the heroics.

Another thing. Aim for brevity again. You need something on the order of a sound bite. It's very hard to make something truly memorable in a thousand words as people lose interest long before you get to the good part. Oh, now and then a guy like Abe Lincoln pulls it off with a Gettysburg Address but it isn't all that common—and those weren't his last words, either. Think in terms of the evening news and be succinct.

Appeal to patriotism, if possible. People really like stuff said by soldiers about to die or heroes on their deathbeds. Remember Nathan Hale's brave, "I only regret that I have but one life to give for my country?" Now there's a line people can relate to. It's punchy yet moving, fearless and proud. It's something you might say if they were about to hang you, isn't it? Damn right it is.

It's a good idea to make some notes as you feel Grim's icy fingers clutching your throat. Get out Bartlett's and pore over the thing for ideas. It's perfectly acceptable to plagiarize somebody else's stuff since you can't be expected to compete with professional writers and heroes in the last word department. If you can come up with the last words of some obscure poet and palm them off as your own, why, so much the better.

Some people even send their last words to the press in advance of their death. William Saroyan was dying in '81 and he actually phoned the press and gave them a kind of pre-deathbed quote. He said, "I always knew everybody had to die sometime, but I thought an exception would be made in my case. Now what?"

Technically, of course, these aren't last words at all, are they? Saroyan didn't die immediately after he hung up; in fact, he died about a week later. Surely those weren't his very last words as he must have said things to people in the days that followed, but the point is they're regarded as bona fide last words simply because Saroyan said they were. They appeared that way in Time and on the wire services and that's enough to make them official.

If you have something truly memorable to say and you want to be sure it gets properly recorded with your last words and you want these to be your actual last words, you could say them as the end drew near and then just refuse to say anything else after that. You could live a week like Saroyan and still make your last words good ones in every respect.

If possible, say your last words in public with lots of witnesses nearby. Caesar and his "You, too, Brutus? Then die, Caesar!" is a perfect example of this dodge. Notice the brevity, the tragic overtones. A nice job of ad-libbing which is usually required of such public utterances since these people rarely know in advance they're going to die at that particular moment and they have to improvise.

Add a touch of pathos if you can. O. Henry did so when he was dying in New York and he said, "Raise the shades. I don't want to go home in the dark." Isn't that nicely done? Of course, we'd hardly expect less of such a writer, would we?

Are epitaphs last words? No. Epitaphs are arranged for by others after the fact. Or if the decedent writes his own he usually has composed it in advance and sent it along to the stonecutter before he gets around to uttering his last words. Of course, a person could say something and die immediately and his friends could have those words emblazoned on the stone and you'd have both an epitaph and last words in one. Still, it isn't normally done this way.

It might be a good idea to jot down your last words on a 3X5 card and keep it handy for the grand finale. When you feel yourself slipping into that abyss and see the bright light everyone talks about you can whip out your card and read off your last words serene in the knowledge that they're just as you wanted them.

A further advantage of the 3X5 card is that in the event you're suddenly struck dumb due to a seizure or something, you can just hand the card to cousin Pete and let him read it to the crowd. Be sure to head the card with Last Words so they'll know your intentions.

Okay, so you're in the hospital or local hospice and you're failing fast. People get the word and they hurry to your bedside to see if you might discuss your will on the way out and the place fills with heirs. You've cleverly set the stage for the last act and you're ready for them.

You've chosen appropriate music to provide background. Aim for something suitable for a deathbed scene and try to avoid hard rock or zither music. Try to schedule your departure for evening so you can have some lighted candles as candlelight is flattering to everybody and your guests will appreciate it.

Try to struggle upright as you speak as the effort will add a dramatic air and draw attention to you. Whatever you do don't speak until you have everyone's attention as you'll only get to say these last words once and they'll be lost altogether if the room is abuzz with noisy talk and raucous laughter.

Gaze raptly on the throng, assume an earnest mien, and speak your piece. Try to speak in a soft, feathery voice to add to the somberness and importance of the occasion, but be sure you speak loudly and clearly enough to assure your being heard. A slight tremor in your voice is a nice touch.

Now the tricky part is to time your actual death with your last words and die on cue. If this is done right you should sink back into your pillow and kick the bucket just as you pronounce the very last word. Really good timing immeasurably improves the effect of your words on your listeners and will cement the moment in their memories for years to come.

"By God, Jimmy really nailed 'er, didn't he?"

"I'll say he did. And that death rattle was a beaut, wasn't it?"

"Yep, he timed 'er just right, he did."

"Yeah, Jimmy went out like a pro. Nathan Hale couldn't have done it better."

Once you've said your last words and died, nothing more is required of you. Your time is your own and you may do whatever you like from then on.

Survival Rules
1. Plan ahead for your last words. Don't rely on ad-libs.
2. Have people present as Grim draws near. Last words are futile without listeners to hear them.
3. Invite a bishop to the proceedings as bishops make credible witnesses.
4. Stress accuracy. You can't fix a misquote later.
5. Be brief.
6. Steal something good from Bartlett's.
7. Try for pathos.
8. Use 3X5 cards to prevent any slip-ups.
9. Set the stage. Arrange music, lighting in advance. Rehearse, if possible.
10. Die a timely death. It makes a swell impression.

CHAPTER THIRTY

Funerals, Etc.

In the spring, they say, a young man's thoughts turn to love. Well, in the deep of winter an old-timer's thoughts turn to other things such as making final arrangements, a euphemism for getting ready to kick that well-known bucket. These final arrangements include funerals, casket choices, epitaphs, organ selections, and similar matters.

There are some people who refuse to consider such things on the grounds that they themselves aren't going to die and so don't need to concern themselves with them. Unfortunately, they're wrong, one might even say dead wrong. You can bob and weave all you like but ol' Grim will get you in the end no matter how agile you are.

These people don't make wills because they refuse to think about death. They won't buy life insurance, either. They feel that if they don't think about Grim he won't think about them but they forget it's all computerized nowadays and computers never forget anything. Their names move inexorably toward the top of those printouts and once arrived the jig is up.

We can't help people of this sort. They can't possibly hope to survive old age with their heads in the sand like the proverbial ostrich. While they're bent over with asses skyward Grim is moving in to round them up and he doesn't give a rap whether they bought life insurance and made wills or not. They go just like everybody else.

Anyway, these types needn't concern us, as they wouldn't read this chapter in any case. For the rest, though, there are some things you should know about funerals and allied matters.

Let's start with funerals. As we all know, funerals are for the living; the star player in most funerals doesn't give a damn if he gets a first-class send-off accompanied by memorable oratory, banks of flowers, cheering throngs, lavish accoutrements, limos, and majestic mausoleums or is tossed willy-nilly into a ditch. He just doesn't care.

It's a well-known fact that dead people are past caring. There isn't a single complaint on file anywhere where a dead person has bitched about his accommodations in any way. It just never happens. It's safe to assume that a total lack of complaints indicates that dead people don't care, especially since a lot of them have not done well in this regard.

Take Mozart, for example. Poor Mozart was thrown into a common grave, a pit, actually, along with a lot of unsavory types who died intestate and could afford nothing better. If anyone was entitled to a little respect certainly Mozart was, yet there is no record of his ever complaining.

Look at Cap'n Ahab. Eaten by a whale. An ignominious end, to be sure. But did he complain? Or Van Gogh mad in an asylum and mortally wounded in a wheat field and consigned to a pauper's grave. Any complaints? Or hosts of people lost at sea, burned up in fires, buried under avalanches, blown to smithereens, atomized, disintegrated. Did any of them complain? No, not one.

So remember, we're making final arrangements for people left behind and not the deceased. There's no real need to pay any attention to the deceased's wishes, as he doesn't care once he's achieved that status. People know this and that's why the wishes of the newly deceased are so often ignored.

If you really prefer one thing to another in these matters, it behooves you to set things up before you go to make sure you get what you want. Raymond Chandler lived here in San Diego and he specifically said he wanted to be cremated. When he died in '59 he was buried instead in a pauper's graveyard where he lies to this day. Don't let that happen to you.

If you want a funeral with all the trimmings, arrange the damn thing before you go. Stop down to the local undertaker's and spell it out. Do your homework. And you can start with prices.

Funerals run anywhere from a few hundred bucks to tens of thousands depending on how gullible the customer is and the degree of depravity in the undertaker. It's not uncommon for poverty-stricken widows with five or six small children to pay over the greater part of their late husband's small life insurance policy to a grasping, unprincipled mortician who preys on their guilt and emotional state.

So watch out. That cheap funeral offers little in the way of frills but it may be enough. You get a cardboard box and a plot next to a contaminated earth landfill. There'll be no view at all and few amenities. Your friends will be appalled at the cheap coffin, single lily, abbreviated elegy, scratchy recording of the Funeral March, and total absence of refreshments. Still, what do you care?

Remember, President Eisenhower requested that he be buried in a plain pine box and he was. He felt it was more than adequate and even appropriate for an old soldier and he was right. The man went out with class, by God.

On the other hand, at the top end you get a coffin that'll keep you dry and comfy for decades or longer. Some of them are even air-conditioned and come with a lifetime warranty. You can get coffins made from rare woods and sporting brass handles for easy carrying. They include innerspring mattresses in some and even offer racing stripes on others.

By the way, the whole funeral is centered on the coffin you choose. When you go to the funeral home to sign up you'll be shown a roomful of coffins with lids ajar for your inspection. The undertaker will try to steer you to the upper end of the scale as his profit depends on how much he can get you to spend on the box. Be wary here. He'll cleverly work on your emotions to drive the price up. The scenario could go something like this.

"Yes, well, we have these cardboard coffins here," he says. "They're priced at one-fifty but, frankly, we don't sell many of them. Sometimes a homeless person will buy one or the city will order some for paupers but we only keep them on hand for, you know, special needs."

"Yes, of course," you say, frowning and moving away. Who's going to want a cheap coffin after that?

"Now, this is a nice model," the undertaker says as he moves to a shiny but plain number with silver handles. "It's all real simulated wood and comes with a five year warranty."

"How much is that one?" you ask.

"Two thousand dollars."

"Two grand!" you say. "They go from one-fifty to two grand? Isn't there any middle ground, maybe something without handles?"

"It's got to have handles," he says. "How will the pallbearers carry it without handles?"

"The cardboard one doesn't have any handles," you counter.

"They don't have pallbearers, either," he sneers. "They truck them out on a dolly."

"Oh."

He moves along. "Now, here's one that's all wood. It has brass handles, innerspring mattress, and a headset for piped in music. This one is only six thousand but it's got a money-back guarantee and comes complete with a view lot overlooking the ocean. You also get an eight-man chorus and a bishop performs the elegy."

"A bishop, eh?"

But you see how it goes. The plan is to go in with a firm idea of what you want to spend and stay within those limits. Don't let the guy talk you into more by hinting that you owe it to the deceased's memory or some such crap. Remember, the deceased doesn't (won't) care.

Get everything in writing. Specify the coffin, viewing room charges, plot and tombstone costs, the whole works. Try to get credit, long-term credit, if possible. Where you're going you won't care if the bill's never paid. If you do pay up front, use a credit card so you can stop payment later if everything doesn't go as planned.

As for the funeral itself, we've pretty much covered that earlier. You have little to do. The usual procedure is for the principal to just sort of lie there and try to look composed. Most people know the routine and nobody is likely to ask you to do any more than that. You are expressly asked to do nothing untoward, remember, like suddenly sitting up or grinning at the guests as such behavior would prove unsettling to say the least.

And that's about it.

But what options are there to a full-blown funeral? Do you have to go this route? No, there's always cremation. You won't hear about cremation from the undertaker as he's whisking you through the coffin selection room at the mortuary because cremation is anathema to funeral guys everywhere.

Why? Because there's no money in it, that's why. Remember how I said the cost of funerals is based on the coffin? If you're cremated, you sure as hell don't need a six-grand coffin, do you? Why lay out that kind of money for something you're going to burn?

It happens that cardboard boxes are ideal

for cremation. They tend to burn nicely with little residue and minimal air pollution and are completely recyclable. If you do have pallbearers, the light cardboard won't strain them and make your heirs liable for lawsuits. And best of all, they're cheap.

In fact, you can have a first-rate cremation with all the usual frills for a few hundred bucks. There's no plot to buy as there's nothing to put in one, no viewing-room costs as there are no viewers, no eight-man choruses needed, no banks of flowers, no professional mourners, no expensive hearses. The only expense beyond the cardboard box coffin is a fee to rent the blast furnace and something for a small urn. Some people even forgo the urn and take the ashes away in a cigar box.

One additional cost for cremation that some people elect is to have the ashes thrown from a plane or taken out and dumped at sea but this is optional and even unnecessary. You can leave them on the mantle or fertilize your roses with them or set them out with the trash. Remember, the owner of said ashes doesn't care one way or the other.

There are still other options even cheaper than cremation. One is to donate your body to science. This is not only cheap but actually free. All you do is sign your carcass over to the medical society people and they'll come and retrieve it when you go. You won't even require cab fare.

What do they do with it? Don't ask. Just remember, you won't know or care.

Another little-known option is to hold your own

funeral. It's possible in most states to bury yourself on your own land. (You'll need help with the actual burying, of course, but you know what I mean.) You may need a permit or something and will probably have to get the exact site approved, but you can be planted in the back forty if you're so inclined.

Still another option is to drown in very deep water or vanish on a camping trip in the Rockies or visit one of our nuclear plants when the thing blows up and atomizes everything in range. In such cases there's no body to muck about with and no need to do anything with the deceased. A clear disadvantage here is that few people drown, vanish, or get atomized in just this fashion so not many of us can avail ourselves of such methods.

That's about all there is to it. As you can see, making these so-called final arrangements needn't be the burdensome problem so many people think it is. A little planning, some forethought, and the advice offered herein will see you through the business nicely and with little trauma.

As I said, it matters little in the end.

Survival Rules
1. Don't rely on others; make your own final arrangements.
2. Watch the undertaker as you would a used-car salesman— he has the same goals.
3. Remember, funerals are for the living; dead people don't care.
4. Go with the cheap coffin. If it was good

enough for Ike, it's good enough for you.
5. Forget the view plots, as you'll do little viewing.
6. Choose cremation. It's cheap and you won't be a problem for the environment.
7. Donate your carcass to science. You'll look good and it's free.
8. Remember, none of it matters, anyway.

CHAPTER THIRTY-ONE

The Summing Up

So there you have it, a Boomer's eye view of the rapidly approaching end of the trail. You've run the gamut from start to finish and finished exactly where everybody finishes. Indeed, it's the only finish possible, isn't it?

Have we learned something here? I hope so. If nothing else, we've taken a little time out to scrutinize things, time to ask ourselves some probing questions and take the measure of this thing called old age. We've seen it for what it is and learned something about dealing with it in a sane and rational manner.

For one thing, we've seen how wonderful it is to be old, how lucky we are to number ourselves among the ranks of senior citizens. An old person is one who's managed to live a long time without dying, and who doesn't want to be numbered among those people?

We've analyzed some of the more popular ways people get to be old. Exercise, for example, has been shown to be useful and beneficial within strict limits, but we've also seen it has a dark side and advised against overdoing it. A lot of people may save themselves some grievous harm by reading this book and heeding our advice to give up jogging, weightlifting, and other strenuous activities.

We've examined diet and touted the benefits of restraint in youth and runaway gluttony in old age. People on the wrong side of eighty have little to lose and should cut loose and enjoy themselves while there's still time.

The same holds true for all the so-called vices like smoking, drinking, keeping late hours, fornicating, watching porn movies, and the rest. These activities should be enjoyed by people of all ages, of course, since they're universally esteemed and much desired pastimes, but they're even more important for old-timers who are running out of time and won't be able to indulge 'ere long.

Again, it's safe to do all these things and many more because really old people have nothing to lose. Should a man of eighty-five give up smoking fat cigars on the advice of his physician? Why? So he won't die? Men eighty-five plus are so high on Grim's printouts that it doesn't make a bit of difference whether they smoke or not. I not only urge him to keep on smoking but to increase his daily intake as a means of showing defiance and the devil-may-care attitude of a man who knows what's going on, by God, and doesn't give a damn.

We've explored the wonders of sex and seen how important it is to keep abreast of things sexual, as we get older. Sex is a life-sustaining force, one powerful enough to ensure continued youth in one who continues to get laid often and well. It could even be said that sex is very near being Ponce's famous fountain since people with active libidos are young at heart if not chronologically.

Along the same lines, old people should dress well and keep up their appearance if only to make themselves more desirable as sexual beings. Lucky is the lady who can be a femme fatal into her golden years and turn men's heads like some slip of a thing mesmerizing her young suitors at the annual ball. Show me a woman of any age who doesn't want to be perceived as a sex object and I'll show you a woman who isn't one.

We also recommend taking advantage of developments in science that can make life more interesting or pleasant. Men who need them should sign up for penile implants and do so proudly as it shows a healthy interest in sex and that means the old duffer still has the right stuff. He should also advertise his new donniker so all the widows in nearby condos will know he's back in service and start plying him with cookies and apple pies again.

Or go for Viagra. They say that stuff will resurrect donnikers that haven't been upright in decades and that's good news for men everywhere—and women, too, I might add.

A quick overview of religion has given you insight into the subject formerly possessed by few men on Earth. Old duffers the world over have studied religion for a lifetime and failed to come up with the brilliantly conceived ideas set forth herein. Since nobody knows which religion is the right one, we insure ourselves by signing up for as many as will have us and rely on the odds to make sure at least one of them is the real McCoy.

What's more, by applying the prodigal son rule we can enjoy life to the fullest and still be pretty sure of getting a berth in heaven by converting at death's door. This is wonderful because we get all the benefits of religion without actually inconveniencing ourselves overly much.

We've provided new insights into marriage and divorce and how to deal with grandchildren. All three can provide much happiness and a good deal of trauma in your life, sometimes simultaneously. The key is to see each for what it is and act accordingly. It's also a good idea not to repeat these things any more often than is strictly necessary in order to minimize the risks.

Some of you will profit from our look at driving, especially if some buttinsky relative has turned you in to the cops and had them lift your license. The tips offered will get you back on the road in no time.

We've extolled the value of plastic surgery and urged one and all to have their carcasses redesigned at regular intervals. A little gel in those wrinkles, some sandpapering here and there, a new chin or nose or ear-bobbing work and you can be a new man/woman overnight. By all means, dare to be the new Phyllis Diller of your condo and look forty again.

You've been made aware of the advances in anti-aging science and may add years to your life via shots and dancing with wild voodooists in the moonlight. If all else fails and you're dying anyway, you can try the freezer plan we discussed and hope for better luck down the road.

We've explained the pitfalls of will making and the dangers of avaricious heirs and how to trick them by hinting they're going to inherit your vast estates when you really don't have a dime to leave anybody. This information alone will do much to enhance the quality of your golden years and help make old age tolerable.

We've examined your options as the end draws nigh. You now know how to conduct yourself when you're hauled off to the local old folks' home and abandoned there by your heirs who were pissed off when they found out you were penniless. You've learned how to avoid mind-stopping drugs and plan escapes from the Sunny Dales of the world and regain your rightful place in society. If you hadn't read this book you wouldn't know enough to escape and you'd languish there until Grim came calling.

You know how to shop for funerals now, too. Nobody will con you into buying a ten grand funeral as long as people still make plain pine boxes and that alone is worth many times the price of this book. Even better, you'll opt for cremation and save still more money while demonstrating that you're ecologically aware in the bargain.

Still, there's more. We've looked the Grim Reaper in the face and stared him down. We've learned to sneer at him with open contempt, to refuse to be intimidated. We know we're in a footrace we can't possibly win, a race where second place is death and extermination and non-existence, and we're okay with that because Nature has so decreed it and we're nothing if not part and parcel of Nature and her master plan.

This isn't some sort of heroic defiance as much

as it is a coming to terms with the inevitable. Why rail against the inevitable? Grim wins in the end and nobody cares that the race is fixed or how we feel about it. It is, after all, the only race there is.

Most importantly, we've pointed out the marvelous freedom old people have because of their age. For the first time the senior citizen can do as he pleases without regard for what others may think because old people just don't give a damn anymore. He can be himself, appear eccentric or even half mad, make a spectacle of himself and elicit nothing more than knowing nods and sly winks as people excuse him because he's old.

Of all the lessons contained herein, this one of freedom may well be one of the most important. Time is running out as Grim draws near, meaning changes shades like a chameleon caught in a rainbow and old rules prove meaningless in new circumstances. It's your last chance to be yourself, your very last.

What matters at last is what we do with our time while we're here. That isn't to say we ought to do wondrous things and build personal empires and rise to places of prominence and gain worldwide fame in order to live meaningful lives but merely to live our lives to the fullest and to bask in the light while it's there for us. It's enough to be alive, to dream golden dreams and master our nightmares, to greet life with a ready grin and a knowing nod.

Now that we're old and bent and dangerously close to the top of Grim's printouts, do we know what life is really about? Has anyone come up with the definitive answer? Are geniuses in some think tank about to make a breakthrough and reveal the truth of our existence at last?

No. All we can ever know for certain is that there is this light and we're able to sit up and look around awhile before Grim shows up and snuffs the light and brings back the darkness of our past.

Is there a new light in that new darkness? We hope so. A lot of people are counting on it and even actively working to ensure a place for themselves in this new light. People have a lot of different names for this new well-lighted place and paint different pictures of its landscape, but no one knows exactly what its geography is or where it is or even if it is.

It's odd in a way that we've made such progress and done so many remarkable things and come to understand even the workings of the universe itself and yet these questions remain unanswered and unanswerable.

What we do know, though, is that it's a very special thing to be alive. There are so many things to do, so many thoughts to think, plans to lay, hopes to hope, dreams to dream. All these things can be done as readily by an octogenarian as a teenager, and often better. Life is a precious commodity at any age and maybe even more precious in old age because we've been able to enjoy so much more of it.

The message is, then, that you should rejoice in your old age. You're one of the lucky ones, one of the privileged ones. So what if you need a walker to get around? Or they won't let you drive? Or your attention span is less than your cat's? Who cares? What does matter is that you're alive, you haven't died yet, Grim hasn't called your name.

So all you Boomers out there go on living just as long as you can. Defy your heirs. Laugh at Grim. Undertake new projects. Learn Greek at eighty a la Rome's Cato. Dress spiffily and cut a wide swath through the widows or seduce all available widowers. Have a drink. Think wild thoughts, dream crazy dreams, inhale deeply, grin a hearty grin.

In other words, live! Remember that the world's never seen anything exactly like you before and will never see your exact likeness again once you've gone. You are an original, one of a kind, sui generis. Stick around; the world won't be quite the same place without you.

The End

www.ingramcontent.com/pod-product-compliance
Lightning Source LLC
Chambersburg PA
CBHW051752040426
42446CB00007B/330